Angolan Women Building the Future

Organization of
Angolan Women

Angolan Women Building the Future

From National Liberation to Women's Emancipation

Organization of Angolan Women

Translated by Marga Holness

 Zed Books Ltd., 57 Caledonian Road, London N1 9BU

 Organization of Angolan Women, Luanda, Angola

Angolan Women Building the Future was first published by
the Organization of Angolan Women, Rua Comandante
Gika no. 199, Luanda, Angola, and Zed Books Ltd., 57
Caledonian Road, London N1 9BU in 1984.

Copyright © Organization of Angolan Women, 1984
Translation Copyright © Marga Holness, 1984

Copyedited by Jana Gough
Proofread by A.M. Berrett
Typeset by Jo Marsh
Cover design by Lee Robinson
Photos courtesy DIP/Luanda
Printed by The Pitman Press, Bath

British Library Cataloguing in Publication Data

Angolan women building the future.
  1. Women—Angola—Social conditions
  I. Holness, Marga   II. Organizacao da
Mulher de Angolana
  305.4'2'09673   HQ1805

  ISBN 0-86232-262-6
  ISBN 0-86232-263-4 Pbk

US Distributor
Biblio Distribution Center, 81 Adams Drive, Totowa,
New Jersey, 07512.

Contents

List of Abbreviations   ix

Introduction by Marga Holness   11

PART ONE: ANGOLAN WOMEN: PROBLEMS AND
PROSPECTS   25

1. The Emancipation of Women   27
   The Position of Women in Colonial Society   28
   Women's Role during the National Liberation Struggle   30
   The Struggle for the Emancipation of Women in the
      Present Phase   30
   The Struggle to Change People's Mentality   35

2. Working Women   39
   Equality at Work   39
   Support for Working Mothers   43
   Peasant Women   44
   Mother-and-Child Care   49

3. Women and the Family   53
   General Considerations   53
   Young Women   56
   Unmarried Mothers   59
   Housewives   61
   Sex Education and Family Planning   64
   Abortion   69
   The Problem of Prostitution   71

**PART TWO: THE FIRST CONGRESS OF THE
ORGANIZATION OF ANGOLAN WOMEN**   75

4. President Jose Eduardo dos Santos' Speech at the
   Opening Session   77
   Women's Devotion to the People's Cause   77
   OMA Faces Difficult Tasks   79
   Machismo Still Exists   80
   Internationalism Is Essential   82

5. Report of the National Committee Presented by Ruth
   Neto, National Co-ordinator of OMA   85
   Angolan Women's Rich History of Struggle   86
   OMA's Work Since Independence   93
   The Position of Angolan Women Today   101
   The Problems Still Facing Women Are Many and Varied   110
   OMA's Aims and Tasks   111

6. Closing Speech by Lucio Lara, MPLA-Workers Party
   Central Committee Secretary for Organization   123
   Women Must Be Politically Organized   123
   More Just Conditions in Our Society   125
   The Solidarity of Women the World Over   127

PART THREE: DOCUMENTS   129

7. Resolutions   131
   On the Emancipation of Women   131
   On Working Women   133
   On Women and the Family   135
   On the OMA Statutes   137

8. Statutes of the Organization of Angolan Women   139

Table 1: Women Workers as a Percentage of Total
        Employed Work Force   42
     2: Production Units and Peasant Occupations   45
     3: Land Utilization   46

List of Abbreviations

ANC	African National Congress
CIR	Centre for Revolutionary Instruction
CONCP	Conference of Nationalist Organizations of the Portuguese Colonies
CVAR	Voluntary Corps for Assistance to Refugees
DGS	General Security Directorate (as PIDE was renamed, both abbreviations given because PIDE was the well-known name)
DNPP	People's Police National Directorate
EDIL	Book Distributing (State) Company
FAPLA	People's Armed Forces for the Liberation of Angola
FNLA	National Front for the Liberation of Angola
GDR	German Democratic Republic
JMPLA	Youth of the People's Movement for the Liberation of Angola
MPLA	People's Movement for the Liberation of Angola
ODP	People's Defence Organization
OMA	Organization of Angolan Women
OPA	Agostinho Neto Pioneer Organization
PIDE	International Police for the Defence of the State
SAM	Medical Assistance Service
SIDA	Swedish International Development Agency
SWAPO	South West Africa People's Organization
UN	United Nations
UNDP	United Nations Development Programme
UNESCO	United Nations Educational Scientific and Cultural Organization
UNICEF	United Nations Children's Fund
UNTA	National Union of Angolan Workers
UPA	Union of the People of Angola
WIDF	Women's International Democratic Federation

Introduction
by Marga Holness

The documents published here of the first Congress of the
Organization of Angolan Women (OMA) are an extremely
rich contribution to an understanding of the problems of a
society in transition. Dealing in an absolutely frank, open
and always practical way with the role of women — who
represent perhaps more than half of Angola's adult population — and putting forward concrete proposals aimed at
enabling them to participate fully in the revolutionary
changes taking place in their country, the Congress stands
out as an important landmark.

Above all, it faithfully reflects the complexity of the
social and historical phase through which Angola is passing,
one all too often grossly and even maliciously distorted by
both academics and journalists. Indeed, the women's
question cannot be properly understood without an understanding of its historical and social context. As a result of
the characteristics of Portuguese colonialism in Angola, the
colonial society was greatly distorted: urban pockets of
relatively high development existed alongside a rural
environment where subsistence agriculture predominated,
backward and based on the most rudimentary technology.
From this rural population was recruited the forced labour
used on settler plantations, where mechanization was also
barely known. At the time of independence, therefore,
illiteracy among the Angolan population amounted to an
estimated 85% with a higher incidence among women than
among men. The traditional family system of subsistence
agriculture, the recruitment of male forced labour and the
tendency of men to seek wage labour to pay the colonial
taxes meant that the greatest burden of the most backward

form of production fell on women. Moreover, since education
was neither free nor compulsory, if a child in the family was
to be sent to school, at enormous sacrifice, it was normally
a boy. The girl's traditional role was to play her part in the
household economy and prepare for child-bearing — in other
words, prepare to produce the new working hands which
are the only form of social security under subsistence
conditions.

While large numbers of women appeared to be relegated
to historical stagnation, using rudimentary methods to grow
scant crops, the very ferocity of the colonial system of repression and exploitation was driving people away from their
traditional patterns of life and home regions. Statistics for
1967 show that more than half of all wage-earners were
engaged in forced labour. In the primary sector — representing
agriculture, stockbreeding, forestry, fishing and mining — the
figure was as high as 80%. Peasants were therefore being
forcibly uprooted to serve as cheap labour to enrich the
coffers of the settlers. These settlers were taking over more
and more of the economic activities until then controlled by
Angolans, and starting up industries, especially for the
processing of agricultural products. Meanwhile, Angola's
border provinces became increasingly underpopulated, the
exploitation and oppression under Portuguese colonial rule
causing a continuous flight abroad, especially in the early
sixties. All this was to have a profound effect on traditional
structures and attitudes, creating an Angolan identity, as
opposed to purely local tribal or regional identities.

Such an Angolan identity had long existed in the urban
areas. Towards the end of the nineteenth and in the early
twentieth century — indeed, before the Portuguese colonial-
ists had completed their military conquest of Angola, owing
to continued resistance which spanned four centuries —
intellectuals were already contesting colonialism. Their
writings laid the foundations of the modern form of the
national liberation movement, a movement not based on the
defence of traditionally held lands but on the assertion of a
national identity in the face of foreign occupation.

This point is of crucial importance. The social transformations set in motion in Angola since the armed struggle was
launched in 1961 have been intrinsic to the process of nation-
formation. One such transformation was the uniting of

women and the measures taken to ensure their advancement first in the struggle against colonialism, and subsequently in the struggle for national reconstruction. The interests of women are identified with the interests of the whole people, of the nation. And constraints upon women's full participation in the revolutionary process are clearly seen as detrimental to the advance of the whole people.

When the People's Movement for the Liberation of Angola (MPLA) was founded in 1956, it proclaimed the equality of all Angolans, regardless of ethnic or regional origin, sex or any other factor. This was a progressive declaration, not only in terms of the inequalities entrenched in colonialism, or of the need to unite the entire people to oppose foreign domination. It was also progressive in that it implied a rapid advance from one historical phase to another. By way of contrast, we see the situation in South Africa, where the tribal homelands, or 'Bantustanization', policy runs counter to the historical process of nation-formation. It inevitably deepens racial, ethnic and other social inequalities, with incalculable negative effects on the family, and on the opportunities for women, as well as men, to derive equal benefit from the achievements of the twentieth century. As in all cases where historical progress is frozen or put into reverse, women tend to suffer the most. They are the most oppressed of the oppressed; theirs is a twofold burden, since the enforced preservation of those structures that prevent national unity carries with it, as a corollary, the preservation of traditionalist concepts and attitudes which place constraints on women's advancement.

African societies in the twentieth century are faced with the need to cover, in as short a space of time as possible, a historical trajectory comparable to that covered by Europe since the start of its industrial revolution. It is a daunting task and, as we have seen, the starting-point has not been an agrarian revolution, as in Europe, but the persistence of primitive agricultural methods co-existing with outcrops of industry directed essentially, until independence, towards meeting external requirements or those of a minority with interests alien to those of the nation. The OMA Congress made a serious attempt to tackle the problems of bringing peasant women into the mainstream of national development, recognizing the need to involve them in new and more

advanced modes of production, and also to make them aware
of this need. Its resolution on the Emancipation of Women
states:

> The Congress recognizes that peasant women have,
> through the ages, been the most exploited and that they
> have least enjoyed social change. It therefore considers
> it indispensable that their consciousness be heightened
> with a view to their increased integration in co-operative
> work, so that they may benefit more from literacy
> campaigns, health education work and any technical
> changes likely to ease their hard work.

This process was started, albeit on a limited scale, during
the national liberation struggle against colonialism, which
was to bring about social and historical changes that have not
yet been sufficiently recognized. The guerrilla war developed
in rural areas of the country, and the bulk of the fighters
were of peasant origin. In the MPLA's liberated areas,
particularly in Cabinda and on the Eastern Front, agricultural
co-operatives, literacy campaigns and health care were
introduced for the first time. The entire nation was represented there — peasants, workers and intellectuals from the
towns, and people from every region of Angola.

The role of women, and the need for them to mobilize on
their specific questions, was recognized from the start. In
1962, one year after the MPLA launched the armed struggle,
OMA was set up. It was not created to oppose men; its
formation stemmed from the fact that the MPLA, as a
progressive movement, recognized the need for the emancipation of women. And it was indeed the national liberation
struggle which gave the greatest impetus to their emancipation. It was in the struggle that women, fighting against a
burden of illiteracy and ignorance far heavier than among men
— fighting also against the traditionalist attitudes of many of
their men comrades — joined the ranks of those who were
prepared to accept every sacrifice and risk in order that their
people should be free from colonial domination.

Angolan women could look to examples of heroines in
their own history, particularly that of Queen Ginga, who in
seventeenth-century Angola united a number of tribes and
led the people's armed resistance against Portuguese colonialism

for 30 years. But only the modern form of the liberation struggle, led by the MPLA, created the conditions for all women to take part on an equal footing with men in the struggle to free the nation.

The report of the National Committee of OMA to the Congress outlines somewhat modestly the role played by Angolan women in the national liberation struggle. That role was a very important one. Not only did women receive military training and take part in combat, they also helped mobilize women to join the struggle and took part in all kinds of tasks intrinsic to it. In the liberated areas, agricultural production was the responsibility of the National Union of Angolan Workers (UNTA) and OMA, and by 1969 more than 40 co-operatives had been set up. In 1973 OMA was awarded Unesco's Nadejda Krupskaya Literacy Award for its work in literacy teaching, an honour usually accorded to countries, not to a woman's organization engaged in a national liberation war.

Commenting on her visit to liberated areas of Angola, Cécile Hugel, Secretary-General of the Women's International Democratic Federation (WIDF), wrote: 'Women participate in that struggle to a very great extent. The women's organization is present everywhere, both in the military bases and among the population. We were able to discuss with their officials and take part in a number of popular meetings.' In the liberated areas Action Committees were set up to run everyday life in the villages. Each committee had to include one member of OMA from among the local population. An interesting factor is that bride-price was abolished in the guerrilla-controlled areas.

A liberation struggle is a far more complex process than is often realized, involving important tasks on the front, in the liberated areas and also in the rear. In Dar es Salaam, the logistical base in independent Tanzania to whose port came ships bearing supplies from friendly countries and organizations, women members of the MPLA and OMA performed all kinds of essential tasks. They wrote radio programmes which were broadcast to Angola, prepared publications for distribution abroad, including an OMA bulletin produced in Portuguese and English, and generally worked to make the Angolan people's struggle known throughout the world and to mobilize international humanitarian aid for the people in the liberated areas, particularly the women and children.

One of those women — and there were many — was Maria P. Supplies unloaded in the port of Dar es Salaam, including beans, rice, soap, medicine and other essentials, had to be taken by truck across Tanzania and Zambia to the Angolan border, a journey of about 3,000 km, much of it over rough and sandy roads. Maria, a slender young woman, learned to drive and service a truck, and used regularly to carry supplies along that vital lifeline. She once said that if a man could drive a truck, so could she.

The liberation struggle was a testing ground where all who took part were called upon to make their utmost effort and develop all their talents and abilities. In this way, under the leadership of a movement opposed to all kinds of discrimination, the emancipated women of an independent Angola started to come into their own in the gruelling tasks of fighting to liberate the entire people.

After independence in 1975 OMA was faced with a new situation. The society it was now working within was far more complex than that of the guerrilla-controlled areas. It had enormous support, however; OMA's membership grew dramatically during the period of the transitional government and the war against the puppet movements and the invading foreign armies that backed them. In the liberated areas the MPLA had been the sole authority in regions beyond the control of the colonial rulers, living in accordance with its own disciplinary code and also performing marriages and divorces under the exceptional circumstances of the war.

When the liberation movement inherited the State structure of the newly independent country, it also inherited all the anachronistic laws still in force until such time as they were replaced by new ones. New laws could not be copied blindly from other countries; it needed the lived experience of the new Angolan society to determine what much of their content would be. This was particularly true of matters affecting women and the family. While the new Constitution enshrined the principles of equality regardless of ethnic origin, sex or other factors, and the Labour Law further confirmed these principles, other matters came up against conservative attitudes which stemmed both from a colonial heritage in which the Catholic Church and the fascist Portuguese State had formed a close alliance, and from traditional Angolan

16

society.

Abortion, for example, was illegal. The battle to legalize it still continues in Catholic countries in Europe. Although traditional methods of contraception and termination of pregnancies were used in Angolan society, traditionalist attitudes regarding the procreative role of women were strongly held, encouraged by the fact that Angola is vastly underpopulated, with an estimated average (according to the 1960 census) of about four inhabitants per square kilometre. OMA countered this argument in the Congress documents: family planning is not a means of population reduction but a means of reducing infant mortality.

The relegation of women to the home and domestic tasks was as much a part of the attitudes of Portugal, a European country whose capitalism was strongly affected by feudal hangovers, as it was of traditionalist Angolan customs. It was not possible simply to introduce new legislation as a way of changing the situation. Experience had to show how to make the requirements of the new society understood by the majority of people, to ensure that not only men but also women realized the need for the kind of historical leap Angola has to make, as we have already seen in respect of its economic development. Social and economic development are inseparable.

Starting from the basic premise that the full emancipation of society is impossible without the emancipation of women, both at work and in the home, it was not enough to persuade men to respect the equality of women. It was also necessary to convince many women themselves of the need to further their education and come out of the home to take part in the mammoth tasks of rebuilding a country devastated by two wars of national liberation and subjected to continued aggression by South Africa and its Angolan hirelings.

During the first years of independence, OMA's main activity was in support of various Government programmes, and it played a vital role in the vaccination and literacy campaigns, for example. Wherever problems concerning women and children required a solution, OMA was present. During the massive South African invasion of Cunene Province, in August 1981, families were dispersed, many men remaining in the trenches until forced to withdraw to safer areas. Among the women whose role was crucial in caring for

the women and children was Angelina Carina, Cunene
Provincial Co-ordinator of OMA and a deputy to the People's
Assembly, Angola's legislative body. From Ngiva, the provincial capital, she led a group of women and children through
South African lines to safety, disguised in clothes taken from
a rubbish heap. At the Congress she was elected to the new
OMA National Committee. In refugee camps, set up during
the 1981 invasion, in Huíla Province, in Chibia, Matala and
elsewhere, OMA was there to help organize supplies for the
displaced persons, to arrange hospitalization for those needing
it and, in general, to do everything possible to alleviate
suffering.

From the time of the 1975 transitional government,
therefore, OMA grew rapidly, with massive support from the
women of the people. On national days and in demonstrations
against Angola's bellicose enemies, OMA's contingents have
always been a lively, enthusiastic and colourful part of the
popular participation, involving women of all ages. Through
its work as a mobilizing body and through its social activities
touched on above, OMA has continued to grow, fully living
up to its role as a mass organization. By 1983, the year of
its First Congress, it had over a million members, 1,014,988
to be precise. This is a remarkable achievement in a country
as large as Angola, whose dispersed total population is
variously estimated at between 6 and 8 million.

OMA, however, had still not tackled in a serious and
systematic way the problems specific to women in society.
The laws of the People's Republic guaranteed non-discrimination as a principle, but time-entrenched practice and attitudes
were another matter. A new family law was still needed, one
taking into account the complexity of a society in which
different forms of union exist — Christian, civil and common
law marriages, rural and urban forms of polygamy. The
problems of rural women, of working women and housewives,
of young women and students — all these required analysis,
guidelines and in some cases laws. It meant taking into
account customs and feelings related to the most basic and
also the most privately experienced fabric of society — the
family unit — within a framework directed towards the
building of an advanced socialist society.

There is no doubt that the seven or so years between
independence and the holding of the Congress were a necessary

period during which experience was gained which was to prove essential in tackling such matters. Had a family law, for example, been brought in immediately after independence, it would doubtless have had shortcomings resulting from a necessarily schematic approach.

Prior to the Congress, meetings were held all over the country to discuss problems specific to women. Meetings of working mothers held in a number of provinces were to provide substantial information on the concerns of this important sector of the working population. Important documents, the 'theses', were written as part of the preparations for the Congress. Examining in depth aspects of the life of women in society, and drawing on historical, economic and social data, the theses were widely discussed and debated. They are reproduced in this volume, shorn only of the synopsis which was appended to each.

Speaking of the theses, President José Eduardo dos Santos said in his speech at the opening of the Congress:

> In this respect, it is important to stress the concerns and problems dominant at the meetings held to discuss the theses on women's right to contraception and therapeutic abortion, their right to pregnancy with medical care and rest; their right to motherhood facilitated by healthy conditions and good food, by the existence of creches and kindergartens, family planning, the solution of childhood problems and so forth. We know that there is no adequate answer to some of these questions in the existing legislation, which in many respects is no longer in keeping with the new social realities. The opinion of this Congress, that of all the women of Angola, on these important matters will be decisive to the drawing up and adoption of laws providing better protection for women, in accordance with the principles defined by our Party.

The Congress was not concerned with 'tokenism'. 'Our objective,' said OMA's National Co-ordinator Ruth Neto — later elected Secretary-General — in her report to the Congress, 'is to raise the economic, social and educational level of Angolan women, so that they may play an increasingly useful part in building a socialist society and in the tasks of national reconstruction.' This participation in national life is seen as the key to women's emancipation. It makes it a part of the struggle to advance the entire people. Indeed, the fact that there are at present only four women on the Central Committee of the MPLA-Workers' Party is a reflection not of male discrimination, but rather of the need for women to advance. In any event, experience elsewhere in the world shows that women can attain the highest office, becoming presidents or prime ministers, without this fact representing an equivalent advance of all women in those societies. In the case of Angola, however, the progress made by women is reflected in the large numbers of women directors of departments and ministries, of women leaders at both communal and municipal level, and most dramatically by the high standard of the documents and proceedings of the OMA Congress itself.

The theme of the Congress was 'Unity, Organization, Development'. The Congress undoubtedly reflected unity, since it represented all the provinces of Angola and women from all walks of life. At least one delegate brought her own interpreter, because she did not speak Portuguese and wanted to make sure that her points were well understood. The delegates had been elected at meetings in every province, following meetings at branch, communal and municipal level. Only in one case, Cunene Province, did the women have to meet in neighbouring Huíla Province because of the continued South African occupation of most of their province. Everyone agreed on the high degree of unanimity achieved by the women at the Congress. There was unanimity in opposing polygamy, for example, which at first sight appears surprising, since it is in many cases part of the subsistence economy. But it is perhaps less surprising when one considers that women account for the bulk of production in that economy. Less unanimity was found on the question of bride-price, regarded by some as representing the purchase of women and by others as bound up with the prestige of a bride and as an essential part of marriage negotiations. It was felt, however, that such questions do not call for legislation. The changing relations of production, and the increased involvement of women in wage-earning employment, enabling them to become economically independent, will ineluctably change social patterns in the countryside, just as they will in towns. These changes are already seen to be taking place. Moreover, social and historical change is occurring within a revolutionary context, which greatly hastens the process. It was also a Congress of international unity, with fraternal delegations from women's organizations from many countries who brought messages of solidarity with their Angolan sisters — from Africa and Asia, from socialist countries, from Latin America, including Nicaragua and El Salvador, and some from Western countries too.

Organizationally the Congress was a triumph. Accommodation, transport and administrative services worked smoothly with simultaneous interpretation at the plenary sessions into Portuguese, English and French, for the benefit of both delegates and foreign guests. There were trips into the countryside, cultural evenings and visits to places of special interest. Foreign guests were impressed by their motorcycle outrider escort of smartly uniformed Angolan policewomen.

Most crucial to the Congress, however, was the question of development. The overriding theme was that women's emancipation was the pre-condition for national development; it was only through active involvement in their country's development that women could achieve true emancipation. This also meant participating in national defence. Subject to constant aggression by South Africa — the biggest military and economic power in Africa — peace is the pre-condition for Angola's development. National defence, therefore, becomes a pre-condition for peace, and hence a major concern for Angolan women, not only through their own participation, but as mothers encouraging their sons to join up and help to defend the country.

The issues discussed in detail at the Congress are contained in the documents published in this book. There is no need, therefore, to elaborate further on them. An interesting aspect of the Congress is that it very pointedly made the women's question the order of the day. In the streets, in homes and indeed throughout the country, people were discussing the issues raised. Husbands were at pains to point out their exemplary attitudes towards their wives. Women were seeing in a new light frustrations and impediments which until then had been ill-defined, but were now posed as national and not personal problems. A qualitative change had taken place.

At the end of the Congress proceedings, which at times continued until late into the night, the final resolutions and statements were read out in full plenary session. The new National Committee of OMA was presented, together with the National Secretariat elected by the Congress. The National Committee represented a broad and representative cross-section of Angolan women from all parts of the country, while those elected to head OMA's various departments were essentially women with proven competence in the fields in which they were going to work. It was generally felt that this would lead to an improvement in OMA's work, since up to now many such posts have been filled by women with enormous enthusiasm but little experience, their more able sisters heading Party and Government departments, with little time left to devote to OMA activities.

Speaking at the closing session, Ruth Neto, the newly elected OMA Secretary-General, said:

> During the proceedings we have spoken and discussed issues that specifically affect women such as voluntary motherhood, since we are the source of life. We reject all old ideas that jeopardize the process of our emancipation. We have debated new questions, some of them surrounded by taboos and prejudices. . . We have decided to fight ideas that relegate women to the role of an object of pleasure, a worker without prospects, an unprepared mother. We have decided to submit to the appropriate bodies recommendations on putting an end to discriminatory concepts, especially as regards the family.

In his closing speech, Lúcio Lara, Central Committee Secretary for Organization, stated:

> The Party and the Government are now in possession of valuable elements which will make it possible to programme action to solve many of the problems that face our women both in the countryside and in the towns, and which will help to establish more just conditions in our society. The correction of some anachronistic laws and combating certain phenomena which affect young women, working mothers, women in the home, pregnant women and children have now become immediate courses of action for Party and Government organs.

This very brief account may give an idea of the importance

of the proceedings of the First Congress of OMA, which
raised in the most serious way problems of vital concern to
all those interested in questions of development, as well as
those concerned specifically with women's role in society.
It was an event unique in Africa and indeed in the world.
Perhaps its most important lesson is that the women's movement, in a progressive society such as Angola, is not waging
a partial struggle, in other words one which is directed
against men. It is a struggle supported by the advanced
thinking of the people's vanguard, in this case the MPLA-
Workers' Party, to free the entire people from all impediments
inherited from a past of oppression and denial, to ensure that
political independence is followed by economic and social
liberation for the entire population — of which women
represent an important part, with their own specific problems
which only they can properly enunciate. Enunciating the
problems does not mean that they have been solved, but it
is an important first step, in this case one which honestly
and openly faces up to the main problems confronted by all
of society.

The final event of the OMA Congress was a gigantic peace
march on 8 March, International Women's Day. The march
started at the newly named Square of the Heroines. Inaugu-
rated on 2 March, Angolan Women's Day, the square honours
the memory of five founder members of OMA, Deolinda
Rodrigues, Lucrécia Paim, Irene Cohen, Engrácia dos Santos
and Teresa Afonso. On 2 March 1967, while on an important
mission in the MPLA's first military region in northern
Angola, these women were captured by the National Front
for the Liberation of Angola (FNLA) and subsequently
murdered in the notorious Kinkuzu camp in Zaire.

Under the main slogan of 'Women demand peace', delegates, guests, Party and Government leaders and a large part
of the population of Luanda marched through the streets
of the capital to the Cidadela, a vast covered sports stadium.
There, after speeches, there was an impressive display of
dancing and gymnastics, the brightly hued clothes and flags
making a blaze of colour against a backdrop of ever-changing
coloured panels held by students, forming vivid patterns
and images. It was a fitting end to a crucially important
national event which, from start to finish, had been a perfect
illustration of the theme 'Unity, Organization, Development'.

It was a fitting end, too, to an event which added a vital new dimension to the struggle for women's rights everywhere in the world.

Marga Holness

Marga Holness has worked with the MPLA and OMA since the time of the guerrilla war against Portuguese colonialism. She translated *Sagrada Esperanca*, the poetry of Agostinho Neto (*Sacred Hope*, Tanzania Publishing House, 1974) her introduction to which has been used in subsequent editions published by the Angolan Writers' Union. After Independence she worked in the office of President Agostinho Neto and later with President José Eduardo dos Santos. She now heads the Angola Information office in London.

PART ONE
Angolan Women: Problems and Prospects

1. The Emancipation of Women

Throughout the history of mankind and up to present times, the development of societies has been related to the division of labour and the struggle between existing social groups to hold and exercise power. In the earliest societies known to us, the female element played a predominant part, owing to the deification of women because of their reproductive capacity, making them venerated and identified with the vital source of things. Hence the matrilinear heredity and descent still found in some African tribes and ethnic groups.

Discrimination against women dates back many centuries. After the disintegration of the primitive community, and with the establishment of private property and the division of society into classes, men secured economic supremacy and, with it, social predominance. Although women had defined rights in traditional societies, their conditions changed with the appearance of colonial society. The burden of women's agricultural labour increased, while the extent and importance of their social labour decreased.

Traditionally, a husband was entitled to the labour of his wives, who had to cultivate crops for their own sustenance and that of their children, and also the husband's crops. The husband became the owner of all surplus produce, and the power that this gave him favoured the entrenchment of private ownership in pre-colonial society. Women could also freely dispose of any surplus produce, and even today this is the only source of cash income for women in rural areas.

With the introduction of industrial cash crops, products traditionally grown for domestic use (rice, maize, cotton) were gradually replaced, not only on small plantations but also on individual plots. Men then kept the earnings from the

Angolan Women Building the Future

sale of industrial crops, leaving women with the meagre
possibility of selling surplus domestic crops. As a result,
women opposed the growing of industrial crops, which meant
the impoverishment of the basic traditional crops from which
they obtained their personal income, since it was they who
had to provide for the family's food needs through
agricultural labour.

Women held a passive position in society, accepting the
status imposed on them by a whole family system based on
private ownership, becoming producers without rights at
the service of the husband-proprietor or the father-proprietor.
The imposed choice of a husband, the exchange of women
for goods and their premature marriage were current practices
which are still common, reflecting the supremacy of men in
traditional society.

The Position of Women in Colonial Society

Under colonialism there was increased exploitation of women's
labour and, therefore, social discrimination. The penetration
of the values of bourgeois colonial society led to the use of
women's labour power in traditional sectors. Those sectors
became essential to the development and ultimate survival of
the new 'mixed' system of production. Under this system,
women's labour power was used for very precise tasks,
especially in the subsistence economy. Obscurantism was
used as a way of dominating women, keeping them in ignorance
and resigned to passivity and servility. Family education
itself played a very important part in preserving that principle.
Only boys could go to school, because woman's place was in
the home to look after her husband and children. Women thus
became men's slaves. The family was the small-scale reflection
of all the contradictions in social development. In bourgeois
colonial society, as in all bourgeois societies, private ownership
left its stamp on the form of family organization. A woman
came to represent an acquisition for man's personal use.

At the ideological level, colonialism used the Church to
propagate the model of the resigned woman whose only
merit was procreation. Although it was essentially in the urban
area that the ideological domination of colonialism made itself
felt, during the latter years of colonial rule desperate attempts

28

were made to take bourgeois values to the rural areas, using the Church for this purpose. Women in the towns were subjected to the model of life inculcated in them. A great number of women were housewives, increasingly excluded from the essential problems of social life. Those who worked in public services, in commerce and so forth were the section of the female population who sought at all costs to achieve social advancement, hastily assimilating the foreign bourgeois model, copying its ways and also its vices. Fashion was one of the means of penetration of the aesthetic and moral values of bourgeois society. Directed particularly at women, it helped to depersonalize and alienate them. Much worse were the use of a woman's body as an object and freely practised prostitution, often a woman's sole means of survival, owing to her low educational level and social consciousness.

Within the monogamous family structure adhered to by the settlers and juridically imposed on Africans, where the equality of men and women was not even formally accepted and where the reproductive function was not regarded as fundamental to social organization, there were situations in which African women were degraded at the same time as they were colonized.

By imposing new forms of labour organization, colonial exploitation had profound effects on the traditional African family. Ideologically and morally speaking, the colonialist contempt for African values, seeing African women as objects of pleasure and using them as such, could not fail to debase the traditionally prevailing moral values.

In this way, factors which in European societies are usually marginal and localized, such as illegitimacy and prostitution, assume great social and political importance in some colonial societies. In terms of social practice, colonialism created conditions for reproducing traditional family relationships which emphasized the negative aspects. The exploitation of women's labour in the traditional family framework was increased because of the need to ensure an economic surplus which subsequently entered mercantile circuits and weakened family structures. African women therefore had an active role to play in production, helping to lessen the social responsibilities of capital through their domestic, craft and productive labour.

Women's Role during the National Liberation Struggle

By fighting alongside men to free their country from the
fascist colonial yoke, Angolan women took the first steps
towards their own emancipation. What was involved at that
time was the liberation of the Angolan people, and women
therefore took an active part in both political and military
activities and consolidated the work of the women's organization — OMA — which played a tremendous role in mobilizing
women, in teaching them literacy and in educating children
in the liberated areas.

We may regard that period simply as a phase in the process
of Angolan women's emancipation, during which women
showed their capacity to carry out all kinds of difficult and
responsible tasks. But it should not be forgotten that apart
from being combatants women are citizens, mothers and
educators of the coming generation. As citizens they need to
be guaranteed the same rights as their partners in all sectors
of national life. As mothers and educators they warrant special
attention from other members of society.

The Struggle for the Emancipation of Women in the Present Phase

Raising the Schooling Level
The principle of equality for men and women in society is
not sufficient to ensure that women are in fact an active
element in their country's development or that they participate equally in decision-making. To achieve equality in its
broadest sense, which implies equal possibilities and the
development of abilities, practical action must be taken to
ensure women's effective participation. Profound changes in
social, political and economic structures are needed as the
fundamental pre-condition for women's involvement in all
spheres of life on an equal basis. These changes will be
essential with the abolition of discrimination against women
in legislation, and they will provide women with the legal
guarantees they need to be able to determine their own
future, first by raising their educational level, secondly by
freely choosing their work and, lastly, by deciding on their
political participation, marriage or divorce and the number of

children they wish to have.

Our country had a colonial heritage of 85% illiteracy, with the largest percentage among women. This led to discrimination against women as regards the opportunities open to them. Relegated to housework, small-scale agriculture, crafts and even small-scale industry, it was difficult for Angolan women to gain access to schooling, on the one hand because of oppression through the family system and, on the other, because their lack of education made them ideal targets for unbridled capitalist exploitation. Many professional activities were closed to them, while the fact that some fields of industry were labelled feminine meant that women provided unskilled and poorly paid labour.

In order to give meaning to the principle of equal opportunity to work, women must have the right to general education, vocational training and continued education in the same way as men, and also to refresher courses enabling them to keep up with new technology.

Since national independence, 297,604 women have become literate in our country, including 108,479 housewives, 105,873 workers and 8,644 members of FAPLA. These figures closely reflect age groups, showing how constant the phenomenon is. Illiteracy and the lack of access to vocational and technical training are the main obstacles to women's involvement in the country's active life.

The lack of conditions enabling girls to learn trades and occupations indispensable to modern production creates a situation where women are available on the labour market. This means that there is no adequate system of vocational training. The constant development of science and technology requires, above all, refresher courses for workers. This is particularly necessary for women wishing to return to work after a long period away from work spent caring for children. Vocational training for women as a whole is possible only at the start of a career.

In our country boys and girls have equal opportunities for general education and everything is done to ensure vocational training for girls, using every possible means to provide education for all social strata. Not only is education free of charge, but study grants and study leave are given to workers engaged in full-time study, guaranteeing that they receive their full pay and other benefits included in the work contract.

In this way, a great number of women have started to study, increasing their occupational skills. Women represent a large percentage of all students in our country.

With one childbirth after another, women have become the slaves of a motherhood which is at one and the same time a source of pride and a punishment. Their selflessness towards their husbands deprives them of any authentic activity. When the only justification in life is motherhood a woman feels let down, having expected too much of marriage. She needs the satisfaction of self-fulfilment in a role which is not exclusively that of a mother. When women feel their worth in their own right, they do not need to prove their worth through excessive childbearing.

Education in the family and school has an important role to play in forming the character of boys and girls, so that they may at an early age learn to take decisions and solve their own problems.

Women's involvement in regular physical exercise, sports and recreation makes for a better physical condition, endowing women with greater capacity and co-ordination and enabling them to have an educative influence on their children and family. It is important to encourage ever more women of all ages to practise sport. The participation of working women in sports activities is enormously beneficial in increasing relations of mutual help and comradeship. Women's involvement in sport has all kinds of positive effects, as an essential and vital activity which prolongs youth, beauty, ability and psychological and physical equilibrium. Among other tasks, OMA needs to encourage mothers to urge their children to practise sport at school, since it permits the formation of habits and customs that influence the development of personality and, generally speaking, social behaviour.

Women and National Reconstruction
By its very nature socialism defends equal rights and provides opportunities for participation and development in political, social, economic and cultural life, eliminating the differential injustices which prevailed during the centuries of class societies in which women had an inferior status.

According to trade union sources, about 122,000 women are engaged in socially useful work in production and services, representing about 24.5% of the country's labour force. These

figures do not take into account the large number of women
working in peasant associations, production co-operatives
and family agriculture. A substantial number of women are
already participating in mass and social organizations, and
women have made an outstanding contribution in the
production of coffee and other commodities in industry,
social work, health, education, urban embellishment and
cleaning campaigns, and in the defence of our territorial
integrity and of the gains of the revolution. The majority
of housewives are still women who live only to solve individual
or family problems, and it is now necessary that they too
contribute with their work, initiative and enthusiasm to the
tasks of national reconstruction.

The life and consciousness of peasant women are gradually
changing as they become involved in co-operative labour and
enthusiastically join literacy and health education campaigns.
Young women are also to be found in production, bringing
keenness and energy to every task, despite a certain resistance
to joining mass organizations and the Party Youth. More
attention should be paid to young women workers, educating
them politically and ideologically to ensure that tomorrow
they will be women dedicated to the cause of the revolution.
It is important to educate young women to combat the
deeply rooted idea that marriage means material security
in life.

Once women start to think in collective terms as regards
reward and privation, they assume their true role in national
reconstruction. It is important for women to understand that
they are working for a better future, not for their own
personal benefit, which means changing their attitude towards
work. Then women so far regarded as invisible workers, whose
production contributes nothing to improving the national
economy, themselves become producers of essential articles.
In the countryside and in towns, in industry, agriculture,
commerce and public services, women must endeavour to
ensure that their work contributes to economic and social
development.

Although the domestic economy is absolutely essential
to the functioning of the economic system, the role of women
involved in it is so greatly underestimated that it becomes
one of the causes of discrimination and leads to their
exclusion from the economically active work force engaged

in national reconstruction. But women's participation in national reconstruction cannot be ensured unless they are emancipated. Indeed, the struggle for emancipation depends on their participation in national reconstruction tasks.

Since they constitute about 50% of our country's population, women have a great responsibility in ensuring a better life for their children, development and national progress.

Equal rights is a fundamental principle of socialist society and will be achieved through women's involvement in labour and in running the economy and the State. It needs to be encouraged and supported wherever there are workers who have the requisite ability and qualities for responsible posts.

Many of the factors which prevent women's participation in national reconstruction are related to educational problems and the lack of social support for working mothers. It is important to understand that the rights women acquire do not represent a personal victory but protection for the family. While, on the one hand, women are more often than not given the responsibility of educating and caring for children, social benefits for women in professional life are not always understood and accepted as they should be. The most difficult thing in the new society is the fact that everything depends on people's consciousness. The aim is to create the new man and woman. Everything is therefore seen in terms of educating people.

When educating women on the importance of socially useful work, we should stress the need for responsibility and rigour in the same way as for men, because equal rights imply equal opportunities and duties, bearing in mind that many situations affecting women, such as pregnancy, childbirth and domestic tasks, are covered by the legislation in force. National reconstruction is the task of one and all, and at a stage where economic organization is the watchword women must, more than ever before, reaffirm their worth and their determination, undertaking production tasks with enthusiasm, discipline, self-denial and revolutionary consciousness. Tempered through socially useful work, Angolan women will have greater strength in fulfilling the requirements of national reconstruction.

Meanwhile, we feel that the task that lies ahead should be to bring ever more female labour into agricultural and

industrial work, as well as into the services. At the same
time, there is a growing need for qualified women, so that in
the more or less distant future — depending on our prompt-
ness and efficiency — women may assume their true role in
the complex tasks of national reconstruction.

Domestic Work

Many women combine domestic work with their professional
activity. The differences between the educational level of
men and women are decreasing. Women's participation in
economic life is on the increase.

Women's involvement in socially useful work is leading
to changes in traditional ideas on motherhood and on the
dependent, submissive and selfless woman. Many domestic
tasks have to be done collectively, creches are being
built and health care and better education provided for the
population as a whole.

We should always bear in mind that mothers of large
families, women employees who are overburdened with
domestic tasks and responsibilities, and housewives solely
responsible for caring for their families unwittingly very often
help to perpetuate the servitude of women.

In this respect, it is of fundamental importance to discuss
and clarify the question of the equality of men and women.
Men and women are not opposite but complementary beings.
One should not refer to the other sex as the opposite sex,
but as the complementary sex. There should be mutual
respect and personal esteem for what each is worth and for
what each is capable of giving.

The Struggle to Change People's Mentality

Fighting Prejudices Inherited from Traditional Society and Bourgeois Colonial Society

> Women are one of the strata of our population who
> have most greatly suffered from the vicissitudes
> of colonial exploitation and the colonialist and
> capitalist mentality that dominated our country . . .
> We must thoroughly revise concepts we have
> inherited from traditional society and bourgeois

and colonial society. Women can no longer be
instruments of labour, decorative figures or sexual
objects.

Report of the Central Committee to the Party's
First Special Congress

As the late Comrade President Dr António Agostinho Neto
said: 'The problem of the liberation of women is extremely
complex. There are various factors involved.' Building a
socialist society, the task we have set ourselves under the
guidance of the MPLA—Workers' Party, requires the conscious
participation of all men and women. It is therefore essential
to prepare the female population of our country, helping
them to overcome the barriers and centuries of backwardness.

The creation of OMA determined the need to educate
women ideologically, to create consciousness as they under-
took increasingly complex activities, and to play an important
role in the building of socialism, thereby representing the
interests and aspirations of this important sector of the
population. Hundreds of women in town and countryside,
aware of the need for their work and prompted by the will
to contribute to economic and social progress, are not
waiting for all the material conditions to be created but
engaging in production, in social and cultural services, thus
starting on the road to full emancipation.

On analysing the problem of women's emancipation, we
come up against crucially important objective factors which
are being gradually overcome with the strength of the socialist
State we are building, and also subjective factors affecting the
consciousness of men and women. The non-discrimination
constitutionally enshrined must be put into effect as rapidly
as possible (Special Party Congress). To this end, there is an
urgent need to start widespread ideological work among
women, from the base to the top, to make them aware of
their role in society, their rights and duties and the ethics of
socialist society.

Women in Defence
In step with national reconstruction, it is our people's duty to
defend our threatened country, a task which has been
occupying a large part of the country's young labour force.
What should be women's contribution to our country's

defence?

During the first and second national liberation struggles, at the most decisive moments in the winning of political independence, women took up arms alongside men, giving great proof of their revolutionary spirit and combativeness.

In our independent country today, Angolan women are prepared to defend our gains and the future. At a time when our territorial integrity is constantly threatened by the racist South African army, Angolan women have an important role to play in defending our threatened country.

In FAPLA, the ODP and the People's Police National Directorate (DNPP), women are already shouldering heavy responsibilities, showing their combat readiness and the technical and ideological level they have attained in performing the honourable task of defending the country, for peace and progress. Mothers with children of military age have the important role of encouraging the young to join the ranks of our army.

On holding our First Congress, it is extremely important that we express the readiness of Angolan women, from Cabinda to the Cunene, to join the fighting ranks, so that we can face up to the war inflicted on us. Educational work among the mothers and relatives of soldiers, to make them understand the true significance of military service, is one of the contributions we pledge to make in encouraging young people to join up.

2. Working Women

Equality at Work

> The problem of the liberation of women is extremely
> complex. There are various factors involved. But we
> must make an effort to make sure that, at a certain
> stage, every woman can have a job, have her
> economic independence, and therefore be able to
> solve all the problems of her life as she pleases, and
> not be obliged, not be subject to following another
> individual, a man, who is sometimes her only
> support and who holds back, hinders and prevents
> women's freedom.
>
> *Comrade President Agostinho Neto*

> Every citizen has the right to work, regardless of
> race, colour, sex, religion or ethnic origin.
>
> *General Labour Law of the People's Republic of*
> *Angola*

Women's struggle for liberation must be seen as a part of the
more general struggle against capitalism, to build socialism
and communism, and never as an isolated struggle directed
against men. A correct understanding and acceptance of this
principle will influence the whole process of women's emancipation and determine whether or not it is possible to make
that just struggle a part of changing the obsolete structures of
oppression. Women, doubly oppressed by capitalist society
and family tradition, must work for liberation in these two
senses.
As stated by the MPLA-Workers' Party in the Central

Committee report to the First Special Congress:

> Women are one of the strata of our population who
> have most greatly suffered from the vicissitudes of
> colonial exploitation and from the colonialist and
> capitalist mentality that has dominated our country.
> This is why we find the highest percentage of illiteracy
> and the lowest level of schooling among women. This in
> itself renders more difficult their integration and
> participation in the new society and in the tasks of
> national reconstruction.

This subjugation under the colonial capitalist system was
aggravated by the domination and submission suffered by
women owing to the patriarchal family structure, in which
woman was regarded as a mere instrument of pleasure,
reproduction and labour.

The taking of political power by the MPLA and the
socialist development option gave women the same constitutional rights as men. The process of women's liberation
therefore assumed characteristics different from those in a
capitalist society, women's struggle centring on creating
conditions permitting their emancipation and direct participation in the national reconstruction process. As already
seen, that process is affected by women's high rate of illiteracy
and low level of schooling and by the acceptance by many
women of submission to men.

The problem is therefore as follows: how is it possible in
the specific conditions of an underdeveloped country, where
a large part of the population is still involved in a subsistence
economy, to define women's struggle for liberation and to
speak of involving women in labour? Does it mean that
peasant women's work in the fields and domestic work are
not taken into account when tackling the problems of
liberating women through work?

The first question has already been answered by setting
women's struggle within the general framework of a new
social and economic order. The problem is how to put that
participation into practice. We all agree that the basic
question, in this respect, is that of wiping out illiteracy and
raising the level of women's schooling and education.

Only study will make it possible to wage a serious

fight against obscurantism and mysticism, since it allows for a scientific understanding of nature and society. In short, it can be stated that it is not correct to speak of liberation if the mind is not freed from obscurantism. We therefore believe that the first stage, which is fundamental to the liberation of women, is to involve them in study, in an open and consistent battle against illiteracy.

It is by increasing their knowledge that women can be properly integrated in production, 'competing with men and thus asserting themselves as an active force in the production process'. Not to see the question in these terms is to make the constitutional equality of the sexes a dead letter and, what is more dangerous, to take the paternalistic attitude of imposing something without being in a position to assume responsibility for it, like involving women in production without paying attention to their degree of academic and professional knowledge, and so forth. In such a situation, women are subjected to even greater conditions of inferiority and submission. The essence of the problem of working women, therefore, is to raise the level of women's scientific knowledge, so that they may in fact attain economic importance.

According to UN statistics for 1970, the number of wage-earning women in the world was about 515 million. This figure represented 34% of world manpower (38% for industrialized countries and 32% for developing countries). According to 1980 estimates, the total female work force in developing countries will exceed the 1970 total work force. The percentage of wage-earning women varies from one country to another and is influenced by social and cultural factors. From 5% in some African countries it rises to 50% in the Soviet Union. Generally speaking, the female work force represents 40% of the total in many socialist European countries, while it varies between 30 and 40% in most of capitalist Europe. According to 1978 statistics, out of a total of 526,785 working people in Angola, 123,779 were women. This female work force was distributed as shown in Table 1.

This amounts to about 20% of the total. Women's participation in the countryside is 25%, as can be seen from the figures for agriculture, livestock and coffee. It should be stressed that the vast majority of working women

Table 1
Women Workers as a Percentage of Total Employed Work
Force

Sector	Total Employed Work Force	Women	%
Transport	47,141	3,624	8
Construction	61,769	3,753	6
Education	61,390	18,086	29
Heavy industry	49,973	3,056	6
Light industry	36,717	7,230	20
Health, administration and services	72,221	22,336	31
Food	75,832	11,926	16
Fisheries and derivatives	17,171	3,021	18
Agriculture and livestock	92,760	17,246	19
Coffee	11,811	33,501	30
Total	*526,785*	*123,779*	*20*

are not included in these figures. In view of the fact that
women represent about half the population, it can be concluded that the percentage of working women is very low, as
a consequence of the low rate of literacy and schooling.

The twofold tasks of working women make it difficult for
them to be involved in the country's social, economic and
political life, preventing them from developing their creative
abilities, limiting their access to technical and vocational
courses and crippling their professional fulfilment. The
fundamental problem is the division of labour in the family.
Up to now women have done more domestic work than men.
When she arrives home, a woman nearly always starts a new
work shift. The complete and true emancipation of women
will necessarily involve the abolition of individual domestic
slavery and the establishment of a wider collective economy.

As regards peasant women, it must be stated that they
have not been given the importance warranted by the great
role they play in the country's economic development. Here
it is more a question of the need to develop the productive
forces in the countryside, which can be achieved only with
the application of new technology and the new organizational
forms planned for the countryside, possible only if the level

of educational, technical and scientific knowledge is raised.

On this basis, the struggle for women's economic and social equality requires that they participate in productive and social work as an important means of ensuring respect for their dignity in society and leading to true emancipation. We therefore believe that this is the context in which the problem of working women should be seen, particularly in a society like our own which has chosen the socialist path for its development.

Support for Working Mothers

Working mothers, meeting in Luanda from 10 to 11 September 1978, at the First Meeting of Working Mothers held on OMA's initiative, recommended a series of measures to protect motherhood, creating the essential conditions for running creches and canteens at workplaces, repealing laws still discriminatory towards women, and taking other steps to alleviate the tasks of mothers and educators. Although many of these measures have already come into force, as for example the Law on the Protection of Motherhood, there are still some difficulties that impede the fulfilment of the lofty social function of mother and worker.

The General Labour Law ensures special rights for working women, but they have not been properly respected by some heads and officials who refuse to take on women in their departments because they might become pregnant, alleging that they are not productive as a result of the pre- and post-natal leave they are granted. It is indeed a fact that a woman works only eight months of a year in which she is pregnant, excluding days off each month to take the child to the doctor and six hours a week for breast-feeding. In other words, a mother works only 162 hours a month.

Such attitudes need to be combated, however, in view of the fact that women are the source of human life and ensure a constant increase in worker and peasant forces for our revolution. In order to ensure that new members of society are healthy and able, protection for motherhood has to be ensured, providing the best possible conditions for women.

Another great subject of debate among workers has been the unstable nature of the female work force, which is very often due to our economic situation. It is important to bear in mind that women are faced with daily difficulties in obtaining essential foodstuffs and articles which make family life easier, such as cookers, refrigerators, washing machines and so forth. It is also necessary to consider the fact that working mothers do both professional and domestic work, amounting to more than 14 hours a day (8 at work and 6 at home), apart from having no weekends or holidays in the home.

Although the number of people's shops has increased, working mothers still experience serious difficulty in obtaining foodstuffs, not only having to be absent from work but sometimes finding nothing to buy when they get to the shop. It is therefore recommended that hours of work be reviewed and co-operatives opened at workplaces.

In order to enable women to take part in productive work without apprehensions, without obliging them to forgo motherhood, or in many cases to give up work itself, women need to be relieved of worries about their children during working hours. In this connection, our Government has made efforts to open a number of creches and kindergartens to make it easier for women to work. Even if not sufficient or adequate, child care centres have a very important role to play in the physical, moral, patriotic, intellectual and aesthetic education of the coming generation, and it is therefore recommended that the building work started on creches should be completed as soon as possible, including, if need be, a voluntary labour campaign to help to build, repair and run them.

It is also necessary to study the problem of some school-age children who attend classes only part of the day and who remain at school without being cared for or provided with activities to keep them occupied. As mentioned in the document on mother-and-child care, OPA should be given this responsibility.

Peasant Women

Because of the social and economic structure of our population and the characteristics of the colonial power, the mechanisms of colonial rule in our country were felt more particularly in the countryside, through slavery, theft of land and taxation. The appearance of avid traders, who also became farmers and who unjustly took over the most productive land, led to the proletarianization of a great part of the male peasant population, caused by the need to earn ever more money to pay taxes. Faced with this situation and the need to defend themselves against a system set up to exploit and oppress them, peasants always tried to maintain their subsistence agriculture, not only to meet their essential needs, but above all in order to accumulate market produce which, in the final analysis, was the only way in which a family could earn the income needed to meet its 'obligations' towards the colonial state.

An assessment of the agricultural sector over the years, abstracted from the 'Total Production of the Country's Economy' and its distribution in society, also allows for an assessment of the living standards of peasants. The unbridled exploitation to which the countryside was subjected during the long colonial night meant that people living there were the most direct targets of slavery in general, and of forced labour in particular. Tables 2 and 3, based on data from the former Agricultural Inquiry Mission for 1971/72, clearly demonstrate the kind of exploitation to which the countryside was subjected, if we bear in mind the areas cultivated, the produce obtained and the archaic implements used for the purpose.

Table 2
Production Units and Peasant Occupations

Production Units

No. of family-type production units	1,198,743
Total area of units	4,710,195 ha
Average area per unit	3.92 ha
Total no. of plots	3,468,904
Average no. of plots per unit	2.9

Peasants Occupation

Exclusively agricultural	752,977 = 62.8%
Mainly agricultural	232,196 = 19.4%
Secondarily agricultural	213,661 = 17.8%

Table 3
Land Utilization

Crop	No. of Peasants Growing Crops (no)	No. of Peasants Growing Crops (%)	Estimated Area Cultivated (ha)	Av. Area per Plot (ha)	Destination Self-use (%)	Destination For Market (%)	Total Production (tonnes)	Production/ Hectare (kg)	Value (escudos)	Value per Unit (escudos)
Wheat	29,165	2.4	30,519	1.046	15.1	84.9	10,145	332	27,362	938
Rice	52,994	4.4	26,061	0.5	18.7	81.3	26,236	1,007	53,311	1,006
Sorghum	69,600	5.8	152,098	2.2	93.7	6.3	27,002	178	31,610	454
Millet	113,394	9.5	132,982	1.2	97.4	7.6	39,202	295	45,185	398
Maize	1,026,343	85.6	1,781,222	1.7	62.2	37.8	686,572	386	802,799	450
Beans	574,308	47.9	245,455	0.4	45.9	54.1	56,178	229	215,925	376
Potatoes	149,761	12.5	33,206	0.2	40.5	49.5	772,136	2,172	87,626	585
Cassava	821,565	68.5	746,718	0.9	77.8	22.2	928,093	1,243	600,592	731
Cotton	21,456	1.8	17,957	0.8	—	100.0	10,853	603	62,306	2,927
Ground-nuts	235,000	19.6	51,908	0.7	50.2	49.8	26,000	501	26,020	110
Coffee	286,353	23.9	178,233	0.6	1.5	98.5	64,085	360	526,385	1,838
Palm oil	142,698	11.9	30,369	0.2	78.7	21.3	1,765	58	8,627	60

The social division of labour almost all over the country differs from area to area, but its markedly underdeveloped character is similar. In the north, men generally grow such permanent crops as coffee, palms and cotton on plots linked with the family. Women, on the other hand, are more involved with subsistence crops like cassava, sweet potatoes and groundnuts. In the southern zone, men cultivate particular plots planted with food, mainly maize, while women maintain themselves by producing food for subsistence on small plots. In the pastoral regions of the south, the normal characteristic form is that of small family groups which are more or less scattered. Agriculture is incipient.

Angola is a predominantly agricultural country with a very high rate of female participation in production, despite the often antiquated methods used. It is women, under sub-human conditions, who produce most of the food consumed by Angolan society and sold in the markets. At the time of independence, only 3% of our country's surface was cultivated. Socially speaking, life in the countryside is hard, and there is a lack of facilities of every kind (transport, drinking water, health services, schools, etc.). Even today women in the rural areas can be seen carrying water in calabashes and using a machete in production. The produce is still ground with a pestle and mortar. In the midst of all these difficulties, it is Angolan women in the rural areas who ensure the production of foodstuffs for subsistence, even producing a surplus for marketing. And it is also peasant women, in rough homes scattered throughout the countryside, who are the pillar of the family, despite the lack of social and production facilities.

All this shows the low level of the productive forces, along with the very small impact new technology has had in the countryside. Despite the recognition of the great role peasant women play in the country's economic development, not enough attention has been paid to solving their fundamental problems, since the changes brought about in the countryside are not as yet visible. This situation makes it more difficult for peasant women to understand the effects of a new society and to accept the innovations already introduced, owing to a high rate of illiteracy and the lack of correct information about new technology.

After 500 years of exploitation, 85% of our people were

illiterate, most of them women living in the countryside. It was therefore with the aim of raising living standards in our country that agriculture was defined as the basis of social and economic development, and industry as the decisive factor. For this reason, from 1978 to 1980 work continued to restore agriculture, which had been largely destroyed and paralysed at the time of independence, and to consolidate its material and technical base while speeding up the transformation of economic relations inherited from colonialism.

There are various projects and programmes for women's development in the rural areas, but many of them are still impracticable and difficult to put into effect for reasons, both objective and subjective, at Party and Government level. The implementation of these goals and programmes must therefore be seen as part of the overall transformation of the rural environment. Activity in the various sectors of the country's political and economic life should at this stage give priority to the countryside, where more than a million families live.

There is therefore a need to seek co-ordinated methods of action in rural areas, to help peasant women, through Party and Government structures, to heighten their degree of technical, scientific and social knowledge, leading to their effective participation in all national reconstruction tasks.

Efforts to this end were made at the Meeting of Working Mothers held in September 1978. During the meeting, attended by representatives of Angolan women from the whole country, there was an in-depth debate on issues concerning peasant women. After studying the difficult working conditions in the countryside as well as in urban areas, the participants recommended the following:

That similar solutions should be found for women workers in the countryside, and especially in agricultural production co-operatives and State economic units, considering that this sector required the attention of the appropriate authorities.

Bearing in mind the need for interaction by women in furthering the raising of their educational level, in order to improve the living conditions of the family and the community as a whole, and to increase the amount of skilled labour in the country, special attention should, in the case of peasant women, be paid to health, education and social services.

It is therefore important to envisage the integration of women in productive and social life in the countryside, so that their full development shall go hand in hand with the development of the productive forces in rural areas. This means that socialist transformation in the countryside (the setting up of associations and co-operatives) depends on heightening the consciousness of women for the tasks in the countryside and bringing them into such organizations.

Steps taken with a view to training able cadres among peasant women are not yet adequate. To remedy this situation, OMA and the appropriate structures must redouble and co-ordinate their efforts to raise the educational, social, economic and political level of peasant women.

Owing to the complexity of problems in the countryside, it would be advisable to find the best possible means of training adults able to deal with the needs of rural areas.

Mother-and-Child Care

In underdeveloped countries children represent about half the total population. The most vulnerable group of the child population are infants up to five years old. Generally speaking, the health services for such children are insufficient and poorly equipped, resulting in a high infant mortality rate estimated at 200/1000. Indeed, up to five years of age children are particularly vulnerable and sensitive. There are factors which can greatly affect and disturb their development and growth, physically, intellectually, emotionally and socially. Despite this fragility, children have an enormous potential, since it is during this period of their lives that their basic personality is formed. The social environment on which they are entirely dependent should therefore be able to meet their basic needs — food, hygiene, health, affection and educational stimulus.

It is usually the mother who looks after a child's health. There is a close biological link between them and they are mutually affected by each other's problems. The under-nourishment and bad health of one has repercussions on the other. Hence the need to care for both. Protecting and promoting the health of children up to the age of five is also

49

a matter of concern, because the biological and psychological needs specifically related to growth have to be met to ensure satisfactory development. Indeed, the adoption of such measures is essential because of the high rate of infant morbidity and mortality resulting from intestinal infections and undernourishment.

When medical care covers the health of both mothers and children, it is known as mother-and-child care. Integrated mother-and-child care should include vaccination for children, advice to mothers on feeding, pre-natal care for pregnant women, advice on child-spacing, family planning, simple forms of treatment, education on clean water and environmental hygiene, and any other matters affecting the health of mother and child.

Mother-and-child care includes pre-natal care. This involves all manner of essentially preventive measures for pregnant women to ensure normal pregnancy and childbirth. It has been proved that pre-natal vigilance reduces mother and child mortality, complications and the number of still-born and premature babies, and increases the number of breast-fed babies. It also helps in the detection of such pregnancy complications as toxaemia, and in planning for the birth, that is, deciding whether the woman can safely have the baby at home or in a hospital, and teaching the woman measures of hygiene to be observed during pregnancy, preparations to be made for the birth and the care of the new-born child.

Child care is especially important. It means supervising the child's health and advising mothers on breast-feeding. Although this is not a problem in most rural communities, it is tending to decrease in urban areas; and child care should also include education on weaning, a period during which a decline in the growth and development of children has been noted in underdeveloped countries, owing to inappropriate foods, and the lack of preventive measures (vaccines, routine examinations, etc.) and of treatment for the diseases they may contract.

There are many factors to be considered when planning a mother-and-child care centre, the most important probably being that it should be easily accessible. Because the majority of the population live in rural areas, mothers cover long distances on foot, with their children on their backs, to reach health centres. Although most mothers do not mind covering many kilometres for something they regard as important, they will not do so very often. This means that health services need to be decentralized and that when a mother goes to a health centre all her needs and those of her children should be dealt with on the same day. These needs may include vaccinations, the assessment of the growth and health of one or more children, pre-natal care if she is again pregnant and, if need be, treatment for common diseases. To offer such integrated and complete care for mothers and children would greatly contribute to the growth and strengthening of a nation.

3. Women and the Family

General Considerations

Engels wrote that the family is a product of the social system and that it always reflects the culture of that system, and also that the family progresses with society and changes with society. This means that over the centuries there have been various types of family and that forms of marriage in different communities are affected by changes in those communities.

Just as the cell is the basic unit of an organism, so the family is the basic unit of society. As a basic unit, the family is of great importance in determining the nature of the structure of society. The evolution of the family has been marked by a constant decrease in the size of the conjugal community between the sexes, leading to the individual sexual union of the monogamous system. The monogamous union based on love is considered the best, since it can be dissolved and allows for successive monogamy, that is to say, people can marry more than once.

Institutions like the family should be seen in terms of the predominant productive relations of each historical era. The family starts as from the moment when two individuals of different sexes come together and decide to live together.

In our country there are still traditional forms of marriage, bride-price and polygamy, in addition to legally registered marriage. Bride-price is an institution whose origins have been lost in time, which is still practised in different regions of our country, and which involves the suitor giving the family of the bride money or goods as a preliminary condition for marriage. The bride-price ceremonies start with the acceptance of the suitor by the bride's parents, followed by a meeting between representatives of both families to decide on the amount of the bride-price and the date of the union. The day finally comes when the bride goes to her husband's house accompanied by two or three relatives who certify whether or not she is a virgin. In some parts of our country the verification of virginity is a cause for great contentment in the community.

Polygamy is a form of marriage in which a man is allowed to marry a number of women. Conscious of the importance of the labour power of women and the children they produce, well-to-do men make sure of such free labour which neither complains nor rebels against exploitation. This is why a woman's fertility is still decisive for marriage, the husband having the right to repudiate the woman and demand the return of the bride-price if she is barren or if he even thinks she is.

However, the predominant form of union in our country is monogamy, although in the towns there is a tendency for a man to have more than one woman. Current practice in towns shows that men tend to imitate the bourgeoisie, making a mockery of marriage through adultery. Some such extra-marital or extra-*de-facto*-union relationships become stable on the birth of children, leading to the disintegration of the initial marriage and even to public quarrels over the 'husband'. What a man may often take to be a result of his personal charm which no woman can resist, or of his important position in society, is nothing more than a reflection of his alienation and the adoption of backward and *macho* concepts which reduce women's historical role to their maternal function of procreation and make them mere decorative objects. Indeed, woman's role in society and in the family, where the exploitation of man by man exists, has been reduced to that of a producer without rights, at the service of her father or husband.

Male supremacy is instilled in people's minds and passively accepted by women themselves. Centuries of domination have brought women to this pass and made them incapable, in most cases, of realizing their own situation. Only changes in the productive relations can change their role in society and in the family. With independence and the socialist option taken by the Angolan people, the conditions have been created for the emancipation of women to become a fact.

Marriage, therefore, should be a relationship of two absolutely equal people, and women should be able freely to choose with whom they want to constitute their family. Equal rights for women are a fundamental principle of socialist society and should be the essential part of a healthy education for young people. The education of children is a most important task for the couple. Concepts of right and wrong are passed on by the family, and although they stem from the innate requirements of human nature, they need to be awakened. When the family does not establish even minimum principles to discipline its members, they do not develop all their abilities and they become adults with a meagre capacity for mastering science and technology. At the same time as they educate their children, parents should seek to increase their own knowledge and understanding of the changes taking place in the world, teaching them the right ideas on peace and solidarity, feelings and concepts which imply honesty and responsibility in their everyday lives.

Socialist society needs a healthy and happy marriage based on love and mutual respect, where children contribute to the happiness of the couple. Equal rights and the dignity of women require that they themselves shall decide how many children they want to have.

Society and the State must live up to their responsibilities, guaranteeing social facilities so that the population as a whole may have a good general education, preparing the young generation for the new relationship between man and woman in marriage, creating services to decrease and ease domestic tasks and recognizing the social function of those tasks.

Partnership and harmonious relations between man and wife create a fraternal climate around them which helps to mould the character of other family members. The family code, for which there is an increasingly urgent need in our country, should not only outline formal principles on marriage, property relations and other legal problems, but should also include advice on the behaviour of partners in the marriage and in the family, so as to prevent negative factors, whether traditional or not, from prevailing and countering the emancipation process.

Society, the State and public institutions have a great

responsibility for the development of the family. Fundamental importance must be attached to full equal rights for men and women under the family law, which, among other things, must guarantee a woman's free and full consent to marriage, combating polygamy, ensuring equal rights as regards the education and training of children, and recognizing the equality of children born in or out of wedlock, especially in respect of descent, inheritance and so forth.

Young Women

Most girls in our country are from their earliest childhood still taught to play exactly the same role as their mothers. From the very start, girls are brought up differently from boys and made to feel inferior. Some girls in towns have a kind of veneer which corresponds to the futile, empty-headed, ignorant and opinionless type of woman with no power of decision-making who allows herself to be influenced by circumstances. The results achieved in their studies leave much to be desired, owing to the scant importance both they and their families attach to their education. This is also reflected in formal education, which consists in observing determined standards of social behaviour.

Relations at family level do not permit girls to acquire a correct concept of their relationship with society. Parents are concerned about the future of their daughters, envisaging only marriage. In the countryside this concern starts when they are still children, and there are even cases of matches between adults and girls of only 11 years old. The bride-price practice continues to govern marriage relations, involving a sum of money or goods given by the suitor to the girl's family as a pre-condition for marriage. Even if the sum demanded by the girl's family is not very high, bride-price cannot be justified as a form of tribute to a woman. It is a reflection of her inferior position in society.

At the First National Youth Conference held in October 1978, the late Comrade President Agostinho Neto told young people:

We have the problem of young girls, most of whom are not yet emancipated. They are dependent on men. What

do many of our girls in towns do when they reach a
certain age? They start to paint their eyes and sit at the
window to see if anyone will look at them. They are
hoping to solve a situation.

In the countryside there is not much of this. It is the
parents themselves who arrange the marriages. The
peasant woman then goes and works as her husband's
servant. They work in production. Therefore, the
problem of the liberation of women is extremely complex. There are various factors involved. But we must
make an effort to make sure that, at a certain stage,
every woman can have a job, have her economic independence, and therefore be able to solve all the problems
of her life as she pleases, and not be obliged, not be
subject to following another individual, a man, who
is sometimes her only support and who hold back,
hinders and prevents women's freedom. This is also
one of the problems of youth. One of the results,
too, would be that there would be no repetition of what
happened during the organization of this conference,
when some young comrades of the male sex tended to
oppose the appointment of young people of the female
sex. A number of discussions were needed for our girls
to take part in this conference.

Now this cannot be. It is because there is no respect
for the female sex.

We always consider that they are inferior, that they
should not take part in political events such as this.
This is one of the consequences of women's dependence,
of their non-emancipation, of their non-freedom, of their
present enslavement, which still is enslavement.

These words clearly illustrate the economic dependence of
young women for whom marriage is the only way out, and
the scant importance attached to their opinions as part of
the youth.

For girls progressively to accede to all levels of planning,
decision-making and execution requires co-ordinated
organizational work. It is not just school, not just the family,
not just mass or Party organizations — all of these should form
an operative educative whole.

It is at home that a child is educated for its future life. During adolescence the social and family environment can either help or hinder proper education for adulthood. The family has an educative function which it exercises not only through the oral transmission of knowledge, but above all by example. When parents have relations of companionship with their children they create a favourable climate for the acceptance of principles and norms of conduct. A healthy home life in which parental authority is accepted and understood will help young people to develop a firm character and a certain self-imposed discipline.

Education for girls at home and at school should combat the tendency of young girls to doll themselves up, looking down on honest work which would ensure them a proper living and hasten their emancipation. Many girls see emancipation as a mechanical process and imitate feminists in capitalist countries.

The use of leisure time and recreation should not be neglected, nor should the legitimate desire to look good. Generally speaking, all young people like to dress well and in an up-to-date way. This is a natural desire shared by young people all over the world, and therefore fashion is not an issue to be avoided. It is not advisable to stop the flow of information on what is happening in the world with regard to clothing, footwear, hairstyles, cosmetics and so forth. Our industry should adapt to our conditions the fashions launched in the big world centres, making seasonally appropriate designs and introducing alterations to make the goods distinctive, so that they may become national creations in keeping with international creations.

OMA must be sensitive to these matters, recommending timely solutions to problems raised by women and especially by young women.

Adolescence is a phase of human life which should be gone through in an untroubled way, achieving maturity with the emotional and psychological balance which makes a young woman receptive to love, friendship and solidarity. The education for life which the whole of society gives young people should naturally be aimed at the self-fulfilment of every individual through socially useful work, as free and equal people who share the same ideal and commitment to serve the masses and the revolution.

Unmarried Mothers

In a country where a *de facto* union is the most common way
of forming a family, most women are unmarried mothers
under the law. Capitalist society penalizes such relationships
through social exclusion. In our country there is no social
discrimination against a couple who live as man and wife.
Some clarification is required, however, on the need for the
legal registration of such unions, because of the innumerable
problems that crop up in life outside the home, not for moral
reasons, but to safeguard mutual interests. The State must
therefore create facilities for the registration of unions
everywhere in the country.

However, we are here considering the case of unmarried
mothers, of those who have children and do not live maritally
with the father. The situation of the unmarried mother is
most often a result of the immaturity of a girl who gets
involved in a relationship without having been forewarned or
who has not definitely decided to have a child under those
circumstances. Without advice, without a full understanding
of her own body, without any established plans for the
future, a girl who does not realize what can happen to her
can easily become an unmarried mother. There is therefore an
urgent need for sex education for young people of both sexes.
Sex should be a subject to be dealt with quite naturally,
fighting the taboos which limit young people's understanding
of their bodies. There are also girls who have a casual relationship with a man and become pregnant although there is no
feeling between them. This is symptomatic of a serious lack
of responsibility. The growing number of unwanted children
threatens the quality of life because, as is well known, the
first requirement for the harmonious development of a child
is to be wanted. Many girls shirk the responsibility of bringing
up a child, abandon the child in a public place or give it to
their parents to look after.

A pregnant girl is always a shock to the family; although
reactions vary from one family to another. Many parents who
never showed any concern about their daughters' social
behaviour react violently to pregnancy, usually demanding
reparations, either monetary or else moral, which is that the
young people should marry. It is necessary to combat the idea
that a girl who becomes pregnant should be obliged to marry

against her will or against the will of the boy. Forced marriages
result in bad relationships between couples, giving rise to
negative feelings and to a bitterness which is usually directed
against the girl, who ends up being blamed for the situation.
At the same time, when unwanted motherhood occurs the
girl feels very alone, and will turn to the boy if she does not
have the support of her family. He in turn will try to shirk his
unexpected responsibilities because he is afraid, and what is a
desperate situation for the girl is an annoying complication
for the boy. If pregnant, a girl should first and foremost
have the support of her family, so that nothing happens
which could harm the child. Instead of repudiating the girl,
the family should finally acknowledge its share of the blame
for what happened, facing up to the new situation calmly.

Very often in cases of pregnancy the two young people
hardly know each other, because of the short space of time
between their first meeting and their having sexual relations.
Hence the need to face the problem of boy-girl relationships
without prejudice. One seldom sees courting couples in our
gardens and avenues. Courting is not out of date, but an
initial stage which prevents people from seeing the sex act
as the only kind of relationship between a man and a woman.
It is a very natural way of establishing a relationship that
makes for a sounder future family life. It also enables young
people to get to know one another and to end the relationship
if they are not compatible. The experience acquired in
courting is something healthy, and even if it becomes a sexual
relationship it does not necessarily entail any commitment.

In some towns in our country, courting in public places is
not seen as something natural. The practice of some public
order officials of reprimanding young couples courting in
public gardens, on beaches or in other public places should
stop immediately. Our policemen are a part of the people,
most of them quite young themselves, and they should be
prepared to understand such things and not to mistake
something normal and natural for an offence against public
morality. The courses provided for them should include
some information about sex. Young people who are punished
and driven out of pleasant places will end up looking for
hiding places and see their relationship as something to be
condemned.

Society and the State need to take measures to provide a

social and legal basis for unmarried mothers and their children. The situation of the mother should not involve any disadvantages. On the contrary, the children of unmarried mothers should be given priority as regards creches and other social benefits. The present family allowance, which is insufficient for a couple, needs to be reviewed, especially as regards one-parent families.

At workplaces, in schools and in neighbourhoods, unmarried mothers should have the support and assistance of UNTA, the MPLA-Party Youth and OMA. Talks about the family should be held in neighbourhoods, schools and so forth, with a view to preparing young people better for their future responsibilities.

Housewives

Women who work only in the home are housewives. The activity of a housewife is confined to the family circle, since she expends all her energy on behalf of her husband and children. A housewife has no wages, no set working hours and no holidays. The husband is the money provider and she the house administrator.

> Notwithstanding all the liberating laws that have been passed, woman continues to be a domestic slave, because petty housework crushes, strangles stultifies and degrades her, chains her to the kitchen and to the nursery, and wastes her labour on barbarously unproductive, petty, nerve-wracking stultifying and crushing drudgery.
>
> *Lenin*

Throughout the history of class societies the fundamental role of women has been to produce labour power, making them responsible for the continuation of the species. A housewife does not sell her labour power or what she produces. Marriage means the confiscation of her invisible labour power and acceptance of the obligation to care for the family, do the shopping and maintain the position held by the husband in society. Domestic work is laborious and tedious and in no way helps the advancement of the person who does it.

Many girls who, because they have no work, enjoy relative independence before they marry, take part in sport and lead a social life, are forced to give up all this after marriage and devote themselves to the home. Marriage, whether traditional or not, is a new stage in the life of a woman after which she either does or does not become a housewife. In the mind of the bridegroom, apart from love and desire, is the idea that from now on he will have someone to look after him, his clothes, his house and his children. Meaning well, he may say that he is going to help his wife, whereas what is needed is that he share the domestic tasks.

In colonial society the marriage ceremony itself, especially the religious ceremony, clearly defined the position of each spouse in the home. The woman was advised to look after the home and be faithful to the husband, while the husband was the protector of the family. A speech made at a given psychological moment can be very effective. Before a large number of witnesses, the authorities endorsed the 'chief' and told the woman to treat property and children with respect, devotion and fidelity.

The socialist State protects and furthers marriage and the family, obliging the spouses to establish relations that enable both to benefit from the development of their abilities. This implies that the personality of each should be respected, because they have equal rights. And this is precisely what registry officials should tell bridal couples. The registrar should not be just a bureaucrat but a person with a good theoretical understanding of society, the family and the liberation of women. Even today many registrars use un-revolutionary phraseology which is humiliating to women. The official entrusted with registering a marriage, a ceremony attended by a number of witnesses, should speak of the role of the family as a basic cell in society responsible for educating the younger generation, and should speak of women's new role in society, using as a minimal basis the article in the Constitution which states that men and women are equal under the law.

Marital authority based on sex, frequent brutality by the husband and his refusal to treat his wife as an equal, leads to friction and contradictions. Such contradictions sometimes sharpen, resulting in physical violence and the break-up of the marriage. Men in our country behave like chiefs with absolute and unlimited powers. These *macho* feelings are passed on from father to son through the power of example. There are an alarming number of cases in our country of men who brutally beat or kill their partners as a result of a quarrel. Because they have no arguments to offer, they resort to the principle that might is right. The *macho* man is the 'border guard' of the division of labour and makes his presence felt every time that a woman takes a step towards liberation. The *macho* man consistently confirms Engels' statement that in the home 'the husband is the bourgeois and the wife the proletarian'. *Macho* attitudes which give rise to male authoritarianism need to be combated, not by empty words against men, 'as though men were sadistic monsters who take pleasure in oppressing women', since this would involve women in a sterile struggle which could never be won, but by fighting erroneous concepts and mobilizing women for specific tasks through which they can release their critical sense and creative initiative.

To emancipate women means to make them economically independent and to free them from the slavery of housework which brutalizes and depresses them. It is the process of women ceasing to be producers of invisible labour and becoming producers of socially useful labour that constitutes the essence of their emancipation in our country. What needs to be done is to involve women in socially useful labour, preparing them culturally, scientifically and technically for that purpose.

According to Lenin 'so long as women are not called upon not only to take part in political life as a whole, but also to engage in continuous and general civic work, there can be no socialism, nor even full and lasting democracy'.

It is important to make women leave the four walls of their houses, but not to become petty traders, as often happens nowadays with women fuelling the black market and exploitation, living lives imbued with imperialist values. Women need to engage in socially useful work and must be mobilized for this, so that they can feel the need to take part in specific tasks and be active agents of social change.

Organizing women raises a number of questions, such as the carrying out of tasks traditionally entrusted to them and the care of children. When a woman returns home after a day's work, she is faced with another day's work, and this increases with the number of children she has. Unlike a woman, a man comes home and relaxes, reading the newspaper or

engaging in some other activity that distracts or entertains
him or increases his knowledge, without in most cases feeling
the need to share domestic tasks with his partner. As a rule,
women do not even stop to think about this situation.
Anchored to a culture formed over millennia of discrimination,
they unconsciously cling to traditional feminine values,
looking askance at a husband who politely offers to take
the wife's place in the kitchen or to clean the house. One of
the problems faced in the liberation of women today is that
it is not only men but women themselves who resist any
revolutionary change in their situation.

Our country's economic resources do not as yet allow for
the large-scale socialization of domestic work. Our towns
have not as yet a network of restaurants, laundries and other
establishments to minimize women's dual task. However,
there is no way of achieving complete equality for women
other than transforming the small-scale domestic economy
into a socialist economy.

It is necessary to educate the younger generation without
discrimination, accustoming boys and girls to carry out
domestic tasks on an equal footing, and popularizing the new
ideas on the marriage relationship which presuppose mutual
help with housework and the care of children.

Sex Education and Family Planning

Sex Education

All campaigns on the problem of the quality of life and,
more precisely, on the survival of children, stress the role of
sex education for young people. Indeed, ignorance is held to
be one of the main factors leading to the death of children.
No stronger argument than this would be needed if people's
minds were not so resistant to the scientific knowledge of
their times, because of prejudices crystallized by centuries
of ignorance. Education comprises a number of elements
which make men and women capable of behaving differently
from animals, since their intelligence develops through the
gradual learning of all the moral spiritual, cultural and
educational requisites. Why should questions related to sex
be excluded from the educational process since sex goes
beyond its strictly primary or procreative function to

influence all human activity?

The sexual urge appears with all the basic characteristics of an instinct, that is, a primitive impulse which is both unconscious and directed. The emergence of instinct is accompanied by a real awakening of sensuality, to which the imagination may add all its capricious constructions. During puberty a whole range of pleasures develop which are to differing degrees related to sexuality. When we study the characteristics of the sex life of young people in our own country, we should not set aside things which are regarded as generally applicable to all peoples. It is necessary, however, to make a serious study of sexual practices, and of initiation and circumcision rites in our country. The purpose of the study should not relate to folklore or the revival of unscientific practices, but to making a critical analysis of what is practised and what it represents for young people. Nor should such a study be used by traditionalists who like so much to go on about what is 'African' and what is 'genuine'. We need to know about traditional practices so as progressively to do away with those which are irrational or unscientific.

An educational system presupposes clearly defined goals and the most appropriate methods of attaining them. The educational system in the People's Republic of Angola seeks all-round development with a view to people's self-fulfilment. Sex education should therefore be something quite naturally taught in the classroom, thus eliminating from the outset the sexual problems of adolescence. It would not be difficult to establish a sex education programme for young people as from the first year of secondary school. Meanwhile, educators should be trained to monitor the sexuality of their pupils from infancy onwards. It is necessary to avoid mysteries about sex in the kindergarten. Sexual urges should be analysed along with all other urges requiring satisfaction such as hunger, thirst and tiredness. Educators of small children should follow closely the sexual development of infants, encouraging and promoting the sublimation of various instinctive urges in different ways. In order to have a correct attitude towards the infant's instinctive urges an educator needs first to be freed from prejudices inherited from his or her own education.

It would be difficult to explain to most mothers in our country matters related, for example, to infant sexuality, but if children attend a sex education class and reference is made to that aspect, mothers will be more careful and will not regard children's instinctive urges as signs of congenital perversity which must be punished, making the child develop pathological inhibitions.

Although young people may not subsequently receive the help they need in the family environment, the sex education acquired at school is always important. Special attention should be paid to carrying out the sex education programme in the countryside, starting with practical experience and then broaching the subject scientifically. Knowing how to listen in order to have a positive influence in changing people's thinking should be one of the methods used in rural areas in respect of sex problems. Regular talks should be given in neighbourhoods, villages and health centres, like those already given on pregnancy. A doctor, nurse or midwife would talk on the issue and then answer questions.

Texts should be prepared on biological facts and relationships. Sexual enlightenment is closely bound up with education in socialist morality and the concept of responsibility towards one's fellows.

Family Planning
Family planning consists in freely choosing the space of time between births and the size of the family. Nowadays family planning is regarded as one of the fundamental human rights, because it is a part of preventive medicine. Birth-spacing and limiting the size of the family are today recognized as preventive health measures and an essential aspect of health in the home, helping mothers to enjoy good health and well-being between pregnancies and helping to restore the emotional strength of parents. According to specialists in this field, mothers who risk dangerous pregnancies can be saved if the risk is identified before conception by the family planning services, who may delay or prevent pregnancy. For many women recourse to family planning services is their first contact with preventive health centres, so that through such centres the community starts to look favourably upon preventive medicine.

One must 'welcome contraceptive methods'. This statement was made at the turn of the century and cited by Lenin when considering the question of abortion. Angolan women should also welcome methods which put an end to successive childbirths, physical weakness and everything that harms them and their children.

Family planning is a method of decreasing the danger of infant mortality and not a method of decreasing the birth rate. A woman cannot have a child a year. The infant mortality rate is generally about 45% in cases of babies born to women who have already had four or more pregnancies. At the same time, the mortality rate of babies born to mothers who have had successive pregnancies less than 15 months apart is four times higher than in other cases.

We are fighting to improve the quality of life. The purpose of the liberation struggles and of the struggle for reconstruction has been to provide a better future for our people. The quality of life starts at the time of conception and, if we are to be more profound, it starts with sex education. For this reason, family planning services should be accompanied by parallel sex education programmes.

One of the essential pre-conditions for the harmonious development of a child is that it should be wanted. We must therefore fight to ensure that children who are born are wanted by their parents. If pregnancy is to end in the birth of a live and healthy child, there are innumerable factors which should be present, and the absence of just one of these can prevent the normal development of a pregnancy. Pregnancy involves all the phenomena which, from conception to birth, permit the development and growth of a new individual. Man's desire to be the master of his ability to procreate would appear to be as old as mankind. Ancient documents describe a great variety of birth regulating methods which were progressively replaced by more scientifically acceptable methods until the times of modern contraceptive drugs and intra-uterine devices.

Contraception means all the methods used to prevent a woman from becoming pregnant. The process consists in preventing the egg, which each month leaves the ovary and descends through the fallopian tube, from coming into contact with the spermatozoid which travels up the genital tract to meet it. Contraception can be ensured through various methods, from the so-called 'natural' methods, to recording temperature and the use of actual contraceptives.

Unlike most couples in the countryside or among the poorer strata, a modern couple prefer to have children only when they so wish. Children then cease to be the result of accident and are wanted by the parents, who prepare themselves to welcome them. The problems of unwanted pregnancies are worse for women, especially in the case of adolescents who run health and social risks. The role of contraception in preventing psychological tension is being taken increasingly seriously by psychiatrists. Unwanted pregnancies often lead to abortion, to feelings of guilt and even to having a baby and then abandoning it. The problem of the traumatized baby, recognized as a distinct clinical case, has in recent years been ascribed to unwanted motherhood.

In theory, all mother-and-child care health programmes should include family planning services, which makes it essential for personnel in various specialized fields to work closely with the hospital services. So long as exhaustive programmes cannot be put into effect, small family planning centres could serve two purposes: to play an important role in mother-and-child care and to become the core of pre- and post-natal care and child care.

Family planning involves visits to a doctor, examinations, laboratory tests, the supply of contraceptives and medicines, and subsequent care, as well as education and assistance that can be provided by midwives and other health workers. A midwife can introduce women to family planning during her everyday work. The educational work she does with pregnant women and women receiving post-natal care is extremely important, because it is at such times that her patients are most receptive to the idea of delaying the next pregnancy. Other methods that can be used are community lectures and the mass media. The mass media should publicize the many problems that occur daily in hospitals, such as cases of women who become pregnant every year and give birth to weak or premature babies subject to mortality, morbidity and congenital malformation. They should also point out how unpleasant it is for a woman to spend all her life washing nappies, looking fat, ugly and graceless, and also seriously jeopardizing her own economic freedom, since successive pregnancies prevent her from contributing to national reconstruction. This factor has resulted in preference being given to male workers at workplaces.

In no country can births be regulated if women continue to live in ignorance and obscurantism. Family planning should be regarded as a contribution to, and not as a result of, women's

emancipation. It is in this sense that OMA should concern
itself with family planning. An extensive explanatory campaign
should now be launched and contraceptive methods should be
put within the reach of all women. Traditional concepts
about women's fertility need to be combated. Together with
the ideas of the Party, new ideas need to enter the rural areas
on the relationship between men and women, essentially
reduced up to now to the act of procreation. This does not
involve the love and affection that make two people feel
close. In most cases marriage is reduced to the sex act, which
must always result in children. The use of educational films
in rural areas, showing a different kind of relationship between
men and women, could help young people in the countryside
to see their relationship in a different way, preparing themselves for the time when they have children and creating
conditions for them to survive and to be loved by both
parents. Voluntary motherhood presupposes not only that a
child should be born only when it is wanted, but also that it
should become someone who is wanted.

A complete and intelligently planned child health programme
should include family planning.

Abortion

Abortion is the voluntary or involuntary interruption of
pregnancy. There are few medical and social questions on
which such divergent opinions are held as on abortion. The
right of the foetus to life and the right of the mother to
health, sometimes in fact to life, can come into direct conflict.

Generally speaking, everyone is against abortion. Abortion
is not and never will be something simple and trivial, because
the woman is profoundly affected. No one has an abortion
for sheer pleasure. Abortion is the result of a consummated
act and is the only alternative open to a woman who does not
want more children and has unintentionally become pregnant.
Experience has shown that women have abortions because,
for various reasons, they either cannot or do not want to have
a child. Legal or illegal abortion exists in every country, in
every society, and it has always existed, differing only in the
way it is carried out. Where it is prohibited, abortion is
clandestine. When a woman cannot go to a hospital for an

abortion and does not want to have the child, she goes to a midwife or to a quack who does not always do it under the best conditions. When forced into clandestinity, abortions are carried out under particularly dreadful conditions. In any statistics on maternity there will be a number of cases of unsuccessful abortions which have resulted in a perforated uterus, in bleeding or a bad reaction to an anaesthetic, after which the woman is rushed to an emergency ward. She is sometimes unable to have any more children, or she may even die.

Historically, the struggle for the legalization of abortion comes a few years after women's winning the right to contraception. Women's liberation movements demand legal and free abortion in the interests of the mother's health, of family harmony and of what the couple want. The legalization of abortion is the only way to guarantee that it is carried out under proper conditions. To close one's eyes and act only in unsuccessful cases is immoral. It is a crime. Legalizing abortion is the only acceptable position in a democratic country. The artificial termination of pregnancy within what is considered a scientifically possible period is the right of a woman distressed by an unwanted pregnancy.

The solution to the prevention of pregnancy is not the legalization of abortion, but sex education and family planning. If sex education is included in the theoretical knowledge given to young people at school, it will help them to be responsible about their sex lives. Family planning makes men and women aware of the rules to be observed and the methods to be used when they either want or do not want children, and it also guarantees the child's right to be wanted. If children are the nation's future, they must be wanted by their parents, who must from the very outset give them the material and emotional security indispensable to the harmonious development of a human being. Motherhood should be a free, conscious and responsible act. The legalization of abortion should help not only to bring out into the open a question that cannot be avoided, however much it is prohibited, but also to ensure respect for the fundamental rights of women and children.

The People's Republic of Angola must give women the right to decide when and how often they give birth. Apart from contraceptive methods, it should allow women to

terminate a pregnancy of up to 12 weeks. Abortion, which
has all manner of consequences, both physical and psychological, cannot be a contraceptive method, but an *exceptional*
way of stopping an unwanted pregnancy. The legalization of
abortion does not mean that those who do not want an
abortion are obliged to have one. It means that those who are
faced with this choice can take it under conditions of safety
and dignity.

The World Health Organization approves of abortion under
the following circumstances:

— Mental or physical danger to the mother.
— Serious danger to the child.
— If the woman is under 15 or the pregnancy is a result of
  incest or rape.
— Following the opinion of two specialists.

A number of completely unjustifiable arguments are raised on
the question of abortion. To say that once it were legalized,
hospitals would do nothing but perform abortions seems a
little hasty. If family planning and sex education were available, sexual relations would cease to be a mystery. Once
people are enlightened, they cannot plead ignorance.

The Problem of Prostitution

Engels explains prostitution in the world as a feature of
monogamy (the modern cellular form of society based on
individual sex love). The cause of prostitution is women's
economic dependence on men. As an offshoot of capitalist
society, it affects particularly the classes that do not own the
means of production and there it takes root. Prostitution is
fuelled by those who hold power, by the imperialist monopolies
which inevitably create conditions for its growth. In capitalist
countries prostitution assumes vast proportions, involving
huge numbers of young women and even children who are
exploited in special places for this purpose.

As Lenin said: 'These twofold victims of bourgeois society
are worthy of compassion. In the first place they are victims
of the curse of the system of ownership that governs that
society and apart from this they are victims of moral hypocrisy.'

Indeed, there can be few things more monstrous than sex being so degraded as to be made a profession. There is nothing that so harms people's character as the forced sale and purchase of caresses between two people who have nothing in common. Prostitution deforms people's normal ideas and impoverishes and poisons their minds. It robs human beings of one of their most valuable capacities, that of feeling passionate love, love that enriches the personality through feelings exchanged.

Prostitution as a social feature of monogamy came to our country with colonialism. The arrival of traders and administrators who had left their wives in Portugal, and later of soldiers, introduced into Angola the same forms of prostitution as existed in the colonial power — uneducated and dolled-up women with no profession, living in a special place.

Why did Angolan women prostitute themselves and sell their bodies to the occupiers? Colonialism established its own way of life in towns. The night-clubs and American bars were in no way different from similar places in colonialist towns. European and Brazilian women came to such places, set up camp and catered for the more select clientele. These foreign women were joined by young semi-urbanized Angolan women who copied the ways of the 'professionals'. Young women who prostituted themselves because they had no means of support or survival in towns, and those who discovered an easy way of making money and going to inaccessible places, were joined by others discarded by their families or society because of a premature pregnancy or sexual relations during adolescence. In towns, there were neighbourhoods and buildings which became the scene of those illicit relations and the women established there suffered humiliation and violence. Not only the bachelor or the man who had left his wife behind in his country, but also the married man who lived with his family, would skulk in the night in search of a prostitute.

Prostitution does not automatically disappear with the revolution. On the contrary, periods of transition such as the one we are going through cause all kinds of disruption, resulting in another type of concealed prostitution. Concealed prostitution affects especially young students who make up to men who can make imported goods available to them. One must also bear in mind the many Angolan women who have lived abroad and made prostitution their way of life. In addition, some women prostitute themselves because they are pressed by the food shortages, and accept the proposition of a salesman or shopkeeper in exchange for two more kilos of rice or a tin of powdered milk for the children.

The phenomenon of prostitution needs to be faced with greater realism by the women's organization, the youth organization and the bodies dealing with juvenile problems. Assistance to young girls at school can be rendered by the Party's youth organization, finding the best way of mobilizing and activating young people. A frank and open discussion of sexual problems, without any taboos, can help girls to understand that they are wasting their lives if they use their bodies for lucrative purposes.

The days of prostitution are numbered. Once women are involved in study and in socially useful work, and when economic life in the country is stabilized, the need for some women to prostitute themselves will disappear.

PART TWO
The First Congress of the Organization of Angolan Women

Refugees from South African-occupied Cunene Province

Ruth Neto, elected Secretary-General of OMA at the Congress

A crèche

Literacy class

OMA in demonstration

Agriculture — new methods

Traditional agriculture

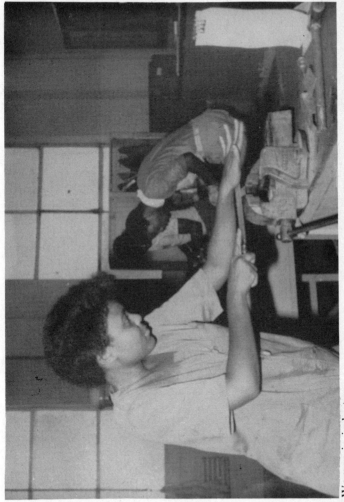

Women in industry

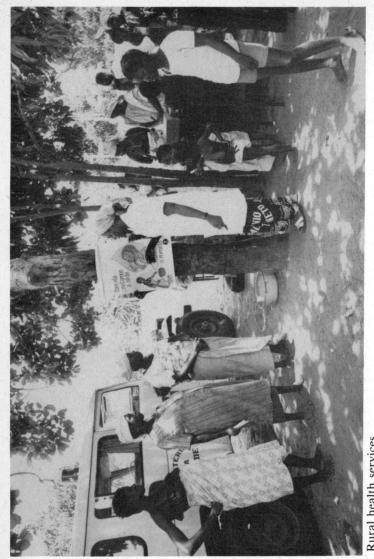

Rural health services

OMA in mass demonstration

Training for the People's Defence Organization (ODP) in Kwanza Norte Province

Women in FAPLA

4. President Jose Eduardo dos Santos' Speech at the Opening Session

Thank you for the invitation extended to me to participate in and speak at the opening session of the First Congress of the Organization of Angolan Women. This Congress, because of its importance and the importance of the themes it is going to tackle and discuss, as well as the fact that it is representative of the national context, is opening up a new phase in the life of our women's organization; it will undoubtedly be a reference point in the difficult and already long process of the emancipation of Angolan women. There has long been a need to hold a national meeting at which Angolan women could analyse in depth and discuss, frankly and without any complex, the problems which most specifically beset women, who are a large and perhaps even the largest part of our population; who, during the colonial period, were those most exploited and oppressed, if we consider that they were subjected not only to colonial domination but also to the authority of their husbands.

Women's Devotion to the People's Cause

The conditions governing the development of the First National Liberation War conducted in the various politico-military regions into which the MPLA divided our immense territory — because of the imperative needs of our struggle — together with difficulties in communication and in ensuring full national representation led OMA, in the course of our history, to promote regional assemblies, enlarged meetings, gatherings and conferences at which the problems of women in our society were debated. They outlined some solutions and, what was more important, defined the role of patriotic and revolutionary women who, alongside their menfolk, played an active part in the national liberation struggle as guerrillas, educators, mothers, leaders or officials. There are many women comrades who promoted that valid work on behalf of our people. They have always drawn inspiration from the example of our ancestors who knew how to fight and how to die with dignity for the ideals of independence, freedom and unity.

In the history of our ancestors, both in the phase of resistance to Portuguese colonialism and in our contemporary history, we find brilliant examples of courage, patriotism and total devotion to the people's cause. One can never sufficiently evoke and stress the exemplary nature of the revolutionary activity of the first OMA militants, particularly that of one of its founders, Comrade Deolinda Rodrigues, as well as that of other heroines such as Teresa, Irene, Engrácia, Lucrécia and so many other anonymous women of our people who, through their selflessness, dedication and spirit of self-sacrifice, helped to lay the foundations for the new society we want to build.

The conditions under which we are waging our struggle for national reconstruction and socialism open up new prospects for ample work among the masses of the people as a whole, and the female population in particular. Using all present possibilities to ensure that women are politically organized and educated for the tasks of OMA, national reconstruction and our country's defence, is a great challenge to our ability and intelligence.

The preparatory phase of the Congress aroused great enthusiasm and has already created great expectations in all women who want to contribute to the solution of the problems which concern us and which have been courageously stated. The theses put forward for discussion, and the intense activity during the preparatory phase, have shown the enthusiasm and revolutionary commitment of all participants and their interest in seeing some of the more sensitive problems of our society solved.

There is proof of appreciable courage and maturity in the in-depth analysis of themes long regarded as untouchable issues, artificially justified by all kinds of prejudice or engulfed in a kind of obscurantism which has greatly contributed to the exclusion and oppression of women even today.

OMA Faces Difficult Tasks

OMA must not, however, allow itself to be lulled by the results
already achieved following the important work done, but must
on the contrary seek increasingly to improve its organizational
structures, its practical working methods and capacity to
mobilize and organize, so as to ensure growing participation
in the revolutionary process by all Angolan women, whatever
their origin, beliefs or educational level. I am certain that this
Congress will make it possible to eliminate some of the
Organization's negative aspects, to ensure that a step forward
is made. To educate, mobilize and organize the largest possible
number of women is the great target to be attained. As a mass
organization, OMA needs to be sufficiently flexible and broad
for all women to relate within it on a basis of equality,
freedom, frankness and comradeship.

As already stated, women were those most exploited and
discriminated against during the colonial era. Reduced to
being objects of pleasure and cheap labour, women were
always hampered in their access to knowledge and science
and were generally confined to the home, to limit themselves
to procreative and domestic functions. It was only women's
participation alongside men, from the earliest moments of
our national liberation struggle, that started to create conditions
for women to recover their dignity and personal responsibility
and to assert themselves as full citizens.

The equal rights won on the battlefield, under the difficult
conditions of guerrilla warfare or in clandestinity, allow
Angolan women today quite rightly to demand of many
compatriots with a conservative and selfish mentality that they
respect women's independence and freedom to take decisions
in personal and family matters, on the basis of the principles
defined by our Party and the legal concepts governing the new
society we want to build. It is not an easy struggle, nor is it a
struggle for women alone; it is the struggle of all progressive
people in our society.

The legal gains already made and formalized in the Constitution are not in themselves sufficient to wipe out centuries of
obscurantism and all the prejudices inherited from colonialism

and traditional society. There is still a certain gap between
the material and formal changes so far effected and certain
practices and mentalities which injure women's rights and
dignity.

Machismo Still Exists

The male authoritarianism that still exists, currently known
as *machismo*, makes it difficult for women to participate
fully in political and organizational work and in the general
effort for production, defence and education. Very often
the basis of this phenomenon lies in male distrust, in retrograde feelings of ownership, the lack of mutual knowledge
and the lack of serious educational work against superstition
and other prejudices, against rumours, intrigue and even
speculation. In this respect the Party and OMA have an important role to play, fighting for the true emancipation of women
and creating conditions for their conscious activity in
production, in raising their educational level, participating
in political and social life and enjoying their legitimate right
to freely consented motherhood.

In this respect, it is important to stress the dominant
concerns and problems at the meetings and talks held to
discuss the theses on women's right to contraception and
therapeutic abortion; their right to pregnancy with medical
care and rest; their right to motherhood facilitated by healthy
conditions and good food, by the existence of creches and
kindergartens, family planning, the solution of children's
problems and so forth. We know that there is no adequate
answer to some of these questions in the existing legislation,
which is in many respects no longer in keeping with the new
social realities. The opinion of this Congress, and that of all
the women of Angola, on these important matters will be
decisive in the drawing up and adoption of laws providing
better protection for women, in accordance with the principles
defined by our Party.

Defending the interests and rights of children must also
be an integral part of the general emancipation effort to be
undertaken with greater vigour. It is unacceptable that in the
new society we want to build there should still be one of the
most aberrant practices of the colonial era: the exploitation

of child labour, mainly in towns, where children said to be relatives provide all kinds of domestic service. So-called abandoned children, who are often war orphans, also deserve greater attention, care and help from us all. We call our young pioneers 'the future of the nation' and this definition implies a responsibility we must all assume and observe in our everyday lives.

Responsibility for the equilibrium and welfare of a growing child brings us to the theme of the couple and parenthood. There is an urgent need to study a new law on family rights in keeping with the new realities we are experiencing. Absolute, unilateral paternal power must be replaced by the power of both parents in respect of children, enabling mothers, too, to guide their children's future.

The question of the dowry and bride-price, historically and culturally explicable as a continuance of traditions deeply rooted in certain sectors of our society, should not be treated lightly. While the Party takes a clear stand against all practices and customs which in any way prevent women from asserting themselves, it is aware that it cannot eliminate such practices and customs overnight merely by issuing a decree. Only the general process of evolution and the development of individual consciousness, through literacy, longer schooling and new social conditions, will eventually eliminate traditions which are not in keeping with scientific concepts of the development of the world and society.

We should not, however, remain indifferent to certain practices amounting to the commercialization of sex which have recently appeared in some of the country's urban areas, where girls follow this practice as a means of acquiring consumer goods which are scarce on the market. It is up to OMA and the Party Youth to make girls aware of the difficult times the country is going through and the need to maintain dignity and honour under all circumstances, devoting themselves to honest and socially useful work. We know that there is a great shortage of essential goods, especially in the towns; but if each one of us were to make a little more effort to ensure increased agricultural and livestock production and to organize transport and trade, I am sure we would solve more than 50% of our problems in the medium term. While we have arable land, water and pasture, there are shortages because of a lack of initiative.

The present situation as regards food supplies is one of the main concerns of our women, since it is usually they who have to put up with the queues and so manage the family budget as to be able to face up to the cost of living. It was in order to meet that concern, which we all share, that our Party leadership and the People's Assembly recently adopted a body of emergency programmes which, among other things, provide for increased food production. I hope that OMA's efforts will be co-ordinated with the efforts of all the bodies called upon to carry out the said emergency programmes, with a view to making the national economy healthier. The fulfilment of all the measures advocated by the Party would also make it possible to create the material conditions for the effective emancipation of women.

The specific aspects of the position of women should not make us lose sight of the overall nature of the country's problems, on the solution of which, in the last analysis, the emancipation of women also depends. Unless we solve the main problems we now face, already defined by the Party as the imperialist war of aggression and the economic and financial crisis, we will not be able to find adequate solutions to women's problems. Women therefore also have an important role to play in solving the main national problems, and OMA, as a mobilizing and organizing force, cannot and must not neglect it. OMA's work in heightening awareness and understanding could contribute to increased production and work discipline, to reduced absenteeism, waste and speculation, and to the patriotic education of youth to fulfil the sacred duty of defending the country.

Internationalism is Essential

Your Congress is taking place at a time when many peoples of Latin America, Asia and Africa are still subject to oppression which seriously affects women's rights, equality, democracy and freedom. In many capitalist countries women are still affected by discrimination, and their labour power is exploited. Only this can explain the fact that although women represent about 50% of the world's population and about 33% of existing labour, they provide 66.6% of the total working hours and in exchange receive only 10% of wages. This crying

injustice must be firmly fought, and the fight must be
strengthened, above all, through solidarity and support for
all women who, in addition to discrimination, are also
bearing the brunt of war, poverty and prejudice.

The voices of our women must make themselves heard
among those of all the progressive and democratic forces in
the world struggling against imperialism, neo-colonialism,
zionism and apartheid, for independence, freedom, social
justice, peace and progress. We must strongly condemn the
occupation of the lands of the Arab peoples in the Middle
East and demand recognition of the Palestinian people's
inalienable right to self-determination and to establish their
own independent state; reaffirm our support for the struggle
of the people of the Sahrawi Arab Democratic Republic;
and condemn the illegal occupation of Namibia and show
our unequivocal solidarity with the Namibian freedom
fighters in general, and in particular with their women's
organization, who are waging a heroic struggle for national
independence. We must condemn the anachronistic apartheid
policy in South Africa and support the struggle led by the
African National Congress (ANC) for freedom, equal rights
and social progress for all the people of South Africa. We must
salute the victories of the peoples and revolutionary forces
in Latin America who are fighting against tyranny and
fascism for complete independence, and for peace and well-
being for their respective peoples.

I should like to end by congratulating all comrades who took
part in preparations for the First OMA Congress on the results
already achieved, which are without any doubt the guarantee
of the success of your proceedings. I wish all delegates active
participation in the debates and, through you, I extend to all
Angolan women, on this 2 March, my congratulations and
sincere wishes for good health and personal happiness.

True to President Neto, let us struggle for economic independ-
ence.
Unity, Organization and Development.
The Struggle Continues!
Victory is Certain!

5. Report of the National Committee Presented by Ruth Neto, National Co-ordinator of OMA

The First OMA Congress has opened its proceedings on the theme 'Unity, Organization, Development': Unity of thought and ideas, Organization in practical activity and mass work, which will necessarily lead to the Development of OMA. This historic event is taking place only a few days after the commemoration of the start of the Angolan people's armed struggle against Portuguese colonialism, and after the twenty-first anniversary of the founding of OMA.

It is with deep feeling, at this solemn moment, that we recall and pay tribute to one who, from the time of OMA's creation, never ceased to give it his full and caring support, encouraging it in difficult times and sharing and rejoicing in our successes, which is why from this hall we answer him: 'Comrade António Agostinho Neto, Immortal Guide of the Angolan People, We are Present!' In his memory, and in that of all patriots, men and women who dedicated their whole lives to the cause of our people's liberation, we ask for a minute of silence and meditation.

Extensive preparatory work has preceded the holding of this Congress. Provincial and local assemblies have given rise to broad and in-depth debates centred on the different aspects of the lives of Angolan women. All of us, those who live in towns and those who live in rural areas, would like here to express very clearly our love for the country of Agostinho Neto and our total confidence in the MPLA-Workers' Party and its leader, Comrade President José Eduardo dos Santos, who through his recent visit to the OMA Headquarters once again showed his great concern and interest in our organization and its revolutionary activity. We also reaffirm our fidelity to

85

the political line of the Party, the defender of peace, of our country's territorial integrity, of our people's welfare and of the complete emancipation of women.

Our objective, through participation and sincere and interested contributions to the work of this Congress, is to raise the economic, social and educational level of Angolan women, so that they may play an increasingly useful part in building a socialist society and in the tasks of national reconstruction. The First OMA Congress is the culmination of a series of experiences our Organization has had in the course of the national liberation struggle and during these seven years of our country's independence, with a view to ensuring the emancipation of women and their full participation in the tasks of reconstruction. The presence of distinguished guests in this hall, of representatives of friendly countries and women's organizations, is proof of solidarity and unshakeable support for the Angolan people and women in their anti-imperialist struggle against exploitation, external dependence and underdevelopment.

Alongside the Angolan people, led by the MPLA, the women of our country, in the ranks of OMA, fully participated in two liberation wars which had the most devastating physical, material and moral consequences. Today women's participation in economic, political, social and cultural life, and the recognition of their dignity as citizens, are due to the efforts and dedication of the finest sons and daughters of our country, who made it possible to establish the People's Republic of Angola. OMA's National Committee salutes and pays tribute to those heroic MPLA and OMA militants. By taking part in the liberation struggle, women made it very clear that they were men's comrades, in no way inferior to them in the common struggle for national independence and against all forms of oppression and injustice.

Angolan Women's Rich History of Struggle

Angola has a rich history of events in which women under arms took part, women who, like Queen Ginga, Deolinda Rodrigues and Helena de Almeida, have through their example been an incentive to the present generation engaged in the struggle to defend our territorial integrity. With the launching

of the armed struggle on 4 February 1961, the Angolan
people, led by the MPLA, directly confronted colonial fascist
military might. And the revolution continued and developed,
mobilizing all strata of people — men, women, the youth,
workers, peasants, students and revolutionary intellectuals.
Women militants in the MPLA felt the need to set up an
organization which would bring together all women in the
national liberation struggle. The purpose of that mass
organization was to mobilize Angolan women patriots for the
tasks of national liberation, defining the ways in which they
would participate, and establishing women's prospects in
the Angolan context. Thus, in September 1961, through
contacts with Angolan women refugees living in Kinshasa
(formerly Léopoldville) who had formed groups of an
essentially social nature, such as the Kuriangó group, political
work started with a view to persuading those compatriots of
the need for a political organization, militant and ready to
meet the requirements of war.

As a result of that activity, in December 1961 the
Organization of the Women of Angola, later to become
OMA, was founded. This opened up excellent prospects for
the full participation of women in the national liberation
struggle. The following watchwords were issued:

> One Objective, Free Angola!
> One Path, United Work!
> One Certainty, Victory!
> United We Shall Win!

Mobilization campaigns were carried out, mainly on the
borders between Angola and the then Congo Brazzaville and
the Congo Republic, subsequently extending to the liberated
areas. OMA's presence was also considerable in MPLA
health and social bodies, such as the Voluntary Corps for
Assistance to Refugees (CVAR), where its members worked
as nurses, first-aid assistants, teachers and administrative
staff. OMA members took part in the agricultural work
needed in order to provide food for refugees. In the course
of the armed struggle contacts were established and developed
outside Angola, and new branches were set up in neighbouring
countries, in Europe and in the liberated areas. In the MPLA's
First Region there were OMA branches which, like the Move-

ment's Action Committees, worked for military, political and social mobilization with a view to supporting the guerrilla struggle waged by the MPLA against the forces of occupation.

At the MPLA's First National Conference, held in December 1962, OMA was represented by a delegation, and after that time our Organization was present at all the conferences, meetings and assemblies held by the MPLA in our country's various liberated areas during the independence war. Angolan women were always esteemed by the MPLA, and they held the same responsible posts as men, at all levels including the Movement's leadership. After the First National Conference, women were represented in the leadership.

In 1963, when the MPLA headquarters were moved from Léopoldville to Brazzaville as a result of imperialism acting through its UPA/FNLA puppet agents, OMA also transferred the centre of its activities to the Republic of Congo. Once again the Organization was represented at an MPLA meeting, the historic Cadres Conference in January 1964, at which resolutions were adopted which were to mark a decisive phase not only for the Movement itself, but for the advance of the armed liberation struggle. As from that date, fighting was reactivated in the Second Region, the Cabinda Front, where OMA had an opportunity to extend its field of action, particularly in mobilizing women in that region and supporting the guerrilla comrades.

To ensure that its members were better prepared for the needs of the war, OMA held its First Seminar on Revolutionary Education at the MPLA's Centre for Revolutionary Instruction (CIR) from 10 October to 7 November 1965. The purpose of the seminar was to assess the situation in the struggle and to increase women's participation. The theme of the seminar was a sentence which was short but significant in terms of its revolutionary content: 'The important thing is not to do what each person wants to do, but what needs to be done to make our liberation struggle advance.' That First Seminar has remained a part of the history of OMA and our people, because it politically, ideologically and militarily prepared a handful of comrades who constituted a nucleus and whose work spread not only to the various OMA branches existing at the time, but to the MPLA's First Region inside our country, and later, in 1966, to the Third Region on the Eastern Front.

During the same period, Angolan women living inside the country under Portuguese colonial fascist occupation carried out no less important work both in urban and in rural areas. Their courage and dedication to the cause of liberation was demonstrated by acts which, though often overlooked or which perhaps passed unnoticed, were nonetheless of the highest value and significance in the general context of the Angolan people's heroic resistance. So many secret messages were carried by them, and so many other items of every kind, medicines and money for the guerrillas in the liberated areas, pamphlets and other propaganda material of the Movement, together with visits to political prisoners and assistance provided for their families. These activities resulted in the imprisonment by the PIDE/DGS of OMA members who, owing to their courage and dedication to the Angolan people's liberation cause, became the targets of ferocious repression at the hands of the thugs of the infamous Portuguese political police. Regardless of age or family situation, many of our comrades fought with dignity and courage, suffering harassment and torture of every kind, their patriotism unshaken.

On the Northern Front and the Eastern Front, in both the liberated areas and those under enemy control, Angolan women gave proof of their political consciousness as patriots and nationalists, confronting the arbitrary repression of the occupying forces bravely and with the greatest self-sacrifice. The guerrilla war carried out by the MPLA always received the greatest logistical, material and moral support from Angolan women as a whole and, in particular, from OMA members.

With the development of the national liberation struggle women took up arms, engaged in combat and joined MPLA military detachments, like the Kamy column, which included Deolinda Rodrigues and four other OMA leaders later murdered by the UPA/FNLA puppets at the sinister Kinkuzu extermination camp. The date 2 March 1967, the day when those five comrades were imprisoned, has been enshrined as Angolan Women's Day. It can never be overemphasized that among the numerous patriots those five beloved daughters of the Angolan people — because of their dedication to the people's cause and their political, ideological and military preparedness — are outstanding examples of MPLA and OMA women guerrilla militants. To secure the release of those valiant comrades, OMA launched an international campaign and the MPLA's Executive Committee appealed to the International Committee of the Red Cross. None of those efforts prevented the barbarous murder of Deolinda, Irene, Engrácia, Lucrécia and Teresa. Their death was not in vain because countless cadres of the Movement and our Organization have followed their example and successfully fulfilled their miss

In 1968 OMA took part in the regional assemblies on the Northern and Eastern Fronts, covering the MPLA's First, Second and Third Regions. Each of those assemblies was of prime importance to the politico-military expansion of the Movement, and it was then that the watchword 'Extend the Armed Struggle to the Whole of Our National Territory' was issued. OMA followed up and put that important directive into practice, setting up a great number of branches as the liberated areas were expanded and consolidated. This activity made itself felt more especially in the Movement's Medical Assistance Service (SAM), in which there were women doctors, nurses, chemical analysts and first-aid assistants. The latter were trained by SAM itself, whose work had an important mobilizing effect on the civilian population in the MPLA's politico-military regions. The presence of women was also noteworthy in the Movement's Radio and Telecommunications Service, where a radio operator course was followed by young militants, some of whom later added to their knowledge in friendly countries. As may be imagined, the work of those comrades was extremely valuable, and even today some of the best cadres are officers in the armed forces in charge of this kind of work. OMA is proud to have among its members cadres who by virtue not only of their technical qualifications, but also of their militancy, are an example of fidelity to the political line of the MPLA-Workers' Party.

At a meeting of leading cadres of the Northern and Eastern Fronts, the presence of women on the Executive Committee was strengthened. Also in 1971, in the same region, OMA's Second Seminar was held with the active participation of Cécile Hugel, then Secretary-General of the WIDF, under the slogan 'Solidarity of the Women of the Whole World with their Fighting Angolan Sisters'. The seminar, which lasted four days, was concerned with the training of grassroots militants for the women's organization in the conditions of the national liberation struggle.

Taking advantage of the visit of the WIDF delegation to the liberated areas on the Eastern Front, Angolan women militants had an opportunity to learn of the experience of women in other countries, especially Vietnam, where they were successfully waging a struggle very similar to ours. Issues such as the organization of practical work, child care and education, hygiene, feeding and clothing were raised and amply debated.

As a result of the seminar's work, OMA adopted new measures to develop its activities, including the setting up of work and education brigades. The seminar had a wide impact, not only domestically but abroad, because it made it possible both to develop our Organization and to make women throughout the world aware of our problems and of the everyday needs of Angolan women, aware of the urgent need for increased solidarity and support for Angolan women fighting for their freedom and dignity.

Putting into effect resolutions of the Second Seminar, and with a view to overcoming the shortage of women cadres to perform the tasks to be carried out both in the MPLA's liberated areas and in the areas under enemy control, OMA decided to create a training centre for its cadres. Apart from this, child care centres had to be set up to help release peasant women from domestic work and permit them to take a more effective part in the struggle.

Delegates to the Third Seminar, at Kitexe II, unanimously decided to set up a centre at Lupa Place (an area bordering on the Eastern Front). It was named after Deolinda, as a tribute to that unforgettable OMA militant. The motto of the centre was 'Learn in order to Teach'. An intensive international campaign was launched at that time to acquire material needed for the work of the centre. International solidarity was not long in making itself felt, in the form of a number of vital donations. In September 1973 the Deolinda Centre got down to hard work, including in its programme such subjects as agricultural production, literacy with classes up to the fourth year, sewing, cooking, hygiene, first aid and ideological education. The work was divided up among Women's brigades named after Deolinda's four companions — Irene, Engrácia, Teresa and Lucrécia. A programme for pre-school-age children was introduced which included reading and writing letters and numbers, drawing, educational games, revolutionary songs and hygiene.

During the Inter-Regional Conference of MPLA militants held in Lundozi in September 1974, the OMA delegates met to discuss problems of the Organization. They adopted statutes and an immediate action programme and decided to transfer the Deolinda Centre inside the country. The meeting also recommended that women who had played an outstanding part in the clandestine struggle should be brought into the OMA leadership. OMA took an active part in the criticism and self-criticism meetings of the Readjustment Movement.

In November 1974 OMA members were part of the official MPLA delegation which arrived in Luanda and of the delegation which attended the signing of the Alvor Agreement with the Portuguese Government.

The late Comrade President Agostinho Neto had a meeting with OMA militants on 25 February 1975, a few days after his arrival in Luanda. That meeting was an especially important one because it was then that the role to be played by Angolan women in the nation's future was outlined. We quote from what was said on that occasion by the Immortal Guide of the Angolan Revolution: 'We want this OMA to be an OMA that faithfully interprets the needs of the female population of Angola.' Our Organization has endeavoured to achieve that goal through its everyday activity from Cabinda to the Cunene.

In the course of the Second National Liberation War, a tragic and heroic period of our history, OMA recorded a remarkable increase in its membership. This caused a violent reaction from the puppet movements in the service of imperialism. Both Unita and the FNLA, with their purported women's movements, using reactionary and lying propaganda, schemed at trying to deflect OMA members. Fulfilling the watchword 'General Popular Resistance', Angolan women in the ranks of the MPLA and OMA actively participated in driving out the puppets and the invading mercenaries, defending the people's gains and our territorial integrity. Among the victims of the bitter fighting, both in the capital and in the provinces, were a large number of women and children. Special mention must be made of Helena de Almeida, buried alive in Bié Province.

OMA's Work Since Independence

It was with the heroic contribution of Angolan women that on 11 November 1975 our country won its national independence, and that on 27 March 1976 our people freed themselves from the invading South African troops. With the proclamation of independence, the work of OMA, clearly accompanying that of the MPLA, was geared to mobilizing Angolan women for the tasks of national reconstruction and recruiting them for the Organization.

In January 1976, after OMA's First National Meeting, when the National Executive Committee was constituted, the 11 comrades elected as officers travelled to the provinces to mobilize and organize women. As the provinces were liberated, OMA went to each one of them to set up leading committees entrusted with carrying out its activities.

In April that year, OMA established an immediate action plan and in November the first Methodological Seminar with provincial representatives was held. At that seminar a number of problems were discussed, revealing the requirements and the difficulties of the Organization, especially the shortage of human and material resources.

In Huíla Province, in May 1977, OMA held the Second National Meeting, during which work was done and future tasks were analysed with a view to bringing ever more women into the many fields of national reconstruction and defence. The meeting adopted the OMA Emulation Plan as a tribute to the First Ordinary Congress of the MPLA.

The constitution of the MPLA as a Workers' Party, on 10 December 1977, represented a qualitative and quantitative leap in the life of the nation. The importance of OMA was again stressed, as was its value as an organization of all Angolan women fighting for complete emancipation and involvement in the tasks of the revolution and of socialist construction. We have endeavoured wholly to fulfil that Party decision, and our work has been directed to helping to solve the problems of women and children, thereby contributing to the welfare of the people as a whole. We have been, and always will be, present wherever the issue is the economic, political, social and cultural development of our beloved country.

It was on this basis that OMA's National Assembly was

held in Malanje from 22 to 25 September 1978. It was a decisive phase in our work, because it made it possible to revise the statutes, restructure the Organization and elect the first National Committee. Mass work was done to mobilize Angolan women and involve them in the tasks set out by the MPLA's First Congress.

Putting into effect the objectives of our Organization, the year 1979 was marked by numerous activities, both nationally and internationally. Because the United Nations decided to make that year the International Year of the Child, OMA, through numerous initiatives and events, made a significant contribution to the national activities related to the UN programme with respect to material, social and cultural assistance for Angolan children. In view of the fact that children's problems assume truly dramatic proportions in our country, because of the difficulties we face militarily, economically and socially, OMA has continued the tasks started on behalf of children in 1979, especially in providing a balanced, healthy and happy life for orphaned, abandoned, displaced and refugee children.

Because we are at war and because each one of us, in carrying out her activities, is at a battle station, OMA has been holding periodic meetings to assess the work done and to plan its contribution, so as to make it more effective in meeting the needs of each moment.

A seminar in Kuito, from 16 to 18 March 1979, provided for a wide-ranging discussion of the work done by the Organization since the National Assembly in Malanje, and OMA's plans and regulations were adopted. That year the seminar decided that great attention should be paid to children. One result was the opening in Luanda of the Nadejda Krupskaya Creche, under the auspices of our Organization. It now accommodates 50 children.

The Impact of War

We cannot underestimate the effects of two liberation wars and the constant destructive attacks by racist South African forces against our country, which has not known peace for the past 22 years.

In view of the situation in the southern part of our continent, on 29 and 30 April 1977 the WIDF, in collaboration with OMA, held a round-table meeting in Luanda on the

theme 'Solidarity with the Women, Children and Peoples of
South Africa, Zimbabwe and Namibia in their Struggle for
National Independence and the Consolidation of Independence,
Democracy, Progressive Development and Peace in Africa'.
During the proceedings of the meeting, special mention was
made not only of the situation in Southern Africa and the
imperialist connivance in acts of aggression committed by
South Africa, but also of the racist Pretoria regime's constant
aggression against Angola. The pressing objective, it was
decided, was the elimination of apartheid, colonialism and
neo-colonialism.

One week after the round-table meeting there was a
genocidal attack on the Angolan villages of Dombondola,
Tchetekere and Kassinga, a criminal act by the South African
racists aimed at intimidating the Angolan people because of
their solidarity with and support for the people of Namibia
and their vanguard organization, the South West Africa
People's Organization (SWAPO). On that occasion OMA's
National Executive Committee addressed a message to
Angolan women recalling the decisions of the recent round-
table meeting and ending by expressing its readiness to fight
alongside the Namibian women and people until victory is
achieved.

It was in 1979 that the Angolan people suffered a terrible
blow in the irreparable loss of their Immortal Guide, the
Founder of the Nation and of the MPLA-Workers' Party,
Comrade President Dr António Agostinho Neto. This tragedy
was a shattering event for OMA and for Angolan women.
The people and the country went into mourning, paying a
heartfelt tribute to the man who had dedicated his life to the
cause of Angola's liberation and who was always unstinting
in his efforts to contribute to the struggle for the emancipation of women and their dignity in society and in the world.
However, the example set by the guide whom the Angolan
people had just lost inspired us; and to honour his memory
OMA closed ranks behind the MPLA-Workers' Party and its
President, Comrade José Eduardo dos Santos, to pursue
the tasks programmed in the interests of the Angolan women,
people and nation.

This has been our work in the 21 years of the Organization's
existence. Of our mistakes we have made victories, because

through them we learn how to improve our work, always adapting it to real existing conditions at each historical moment. Consistently and constructively applying the Organization's statutory principles, we are seeking to structure it in such a way as to ensure that it can correctly guide the struggle towards the goal of building socialism. By combating, eliminating and correcting our errors and shortcomings, let us strengthen unity and discipline, and so contribute to the development of OMA.

As a result of its continually improved work, OMA now has 1,014,988 members distributed in 18 provinces, in 163 municipalities and 386 communes, and organized in 5,595 neighbourhood and village branches.

Despite the many difficulties, particularly the shortage of cadres which obliges some departments to operate without efficient workers to carry out programmed tasks, the demobilization of some women members, and even the slowness of some members in the leadership in applying working methods decided upon, we can say that our activity has been positive as a result of the dedication and selflessness shown by women, by comrades, especially at provincial level.

We make special mention of the OMA members in the war zones who at every moment face the attacks of the South African racists and their puppets in imperialist pay. Unsparing in their efforts and risking their own lives, comrades in those stricken areas, some of them still occupied by the enemy, have responded positively to the guidelines of the MPLA-Workers' Party and of Comrade President José Eduardo dos Santos.

Our work has been put into practice at all levels, in ideology, production, health and social affairs, education, organization, external relations, information and propaganda, and it will be analysed in detail in this report. OMA has held methodological seminars to assess the work done and to plan future activities. It has organized round-table conferences and run literacy and vaccination campaigns. It has taken part in such agricultural activities as the coffee and cotton harvests. It has done social work in mother-and-child care and at the same time organized cadre-training courses, especially at the Huambo Centre, promoting meetings, assemblies and contacts at national, provincial, municipal and communal level.

Because women in rural areas constitute the bulk of the

Organization, it has been OMA's constant concern to give greater support to women in the countryside, helping to set up collective farms equipped with health, education and social facilities. Our Organization is trying to improve the living and working conditions of peasant women, providing them with whatever means we can to facilitate the tough tasks of agriculture.

Two meetings of working mothers have been held at which Angolan women from different sectors of national life have discussed and put forward solutions for some of the daily problems they face as mothers, workers, peasants and intellectuals.

Information and propaganda have been directed towards using the mass media and OMA Bulletin as a means of informing Angolan women of the Organization's directives, publicizing the work done, politicizing women and mobilizing them fully to assume their role in the struggle for involvement in every form of activity and in the defence of our independent and sovereign country.

In the field of foreign affairs, we have followed the line laid down by the MPLA-Workers' Party and sought to inform national, continental and international women's organizations with which we maintain friendly relations about the politico-military situation in our country and the role played by OMA in our society. At the same time we try to learn about and study the experience of women in other countries, particularly those who, like ourselves, are fighting to consolidate and defend their independence and territorial integrity, for the establishment of a just society in which there shall be no exploitation of man by man.

Also in the context of relations with other organizations and other peoples, we cannot fail to mention the internationalist solidarity which, through their mass organization OMA, Angolan women have received from many national and international women's organizations since the start of the armed liberation struggle. Special mention should be made of women's organizations in socialist countries and African countries which have given us shelter and support, and also of democratic and progressive international organizations.

Allow us to refer especially to our friends of the Soviet Women's Committee, the Federation of Cuban Women and

the Revolutionary Union of Congolese Women for the high
level of their co-operation, both before and after our
independence. We should also like to emphasize the activity
of the WIDF and the Pan-African Women's Organization.

International Contacts

In detailing the work done by OMA in external relations,
ideological work, productive and social work, information
and propaganda, and organization, we should like to inform
the Congress that new friendships have been developed and
consolidated with international organizations all over the
world; and that OMA has been able to attend a number of
international conferences and make a number of friendly
working visits.

In October 1975, on the eve of our country's independence,
an OMA delegation left for Berlin to attend the World
Conference for International Women's Year. At that conference OMA denounced the acts of banditry committed
against the Angolan people by the FNLA and Unita bandits.
At the WIDF Congress, held at that same time, OMA called
for the recognition of the MPLA as the sole legitimate
movement capable of leading Angola to just and real
independence.

With the advent of 11 November, and hence of national
independence, a new phase in the struggle started. Following
the guidelines of its vanguard, the MPLA, OMA faced national
reconstruction tasks with new prospects for its organizational
work. In October 1976 an OMA delegation visited 11 West
European countries in order to tell the world about the racist
invasion of our country, the goal we set ourselves of building
scientific socialism in Angola, and our wish to establish
relations with all countries in the world on the basis of
respect for the universally recognized principles of peaceful
co-existence between peoples, respect for sovereignty and
territorial integrity, non-interference in internal affairs,
and mutual advantage.

There were a number of trips and working visits during
which delegations from our Organization, at congresses,
conferences, seminars and other meetings, had occasion to
describe the realities of our country and the activity of
Angolan women. For instance, we took part in the Third
Preparatory Conference for the World Conference on

Children. held in Algiers in May 1979.

As regards the Decade for Women, we should mention the round-table conference held in Luanda and two marches for peace and solidarity with the women of Namibia and South Africa, in August 1981 and March 1982. Those marches, which took place throughout the country, proved a great success, and not only the population of our country but a large number of foreign citizens resident in the People's Republic of Angola took part in them.

Also among the activities related to the UN Decade, in 1980 OMA was represented at the World Conference on the Decade for Women held in Copenhagen, and at the Forum of Non-Governmental Organizations, in a delegation representing our country and in the WIDF delegation respectively.

Also representing the WIDF, OMA led two delegations to Asian countries, in 1980 to the Philippines (Seminar on the Training of Rural Women Leaders in Socio-Economic Development), and in April 1981 to a meeting in India of the Women for Peace and Disarmament working group, in preparation for the World Conference of Women.

In support of the women of our continent who are fighting colonialism and apartheid, OMA took part in the Brussels Conference in Solidarity with the Women of South Africa and Namibia, in May 1982.

At the national level, OMA provided facilities for the ANC Women's Section to hold its Congress in Luanda, and for the SWAPO Women's Congress held in Kwanza Sul Province.

The Week of Solidarity with the Women of South Africa and Namibia, which is held annually from 31 July to 9 August and which culminates in South African Women's Day, is always an occasion for mass demonstrations in our country.

The struggle of the Sahrawi people against the Moroccan occupiers has OMA's full support and admiration. Our sisters in the Sahrawi Arab Democratic Republic can testify to the consistent solidarity of Angolan women.

Our internationalist solidarity extends to the women of the whole world who, in Latin America, in the Middle East, in Asia and in capitalist countries, are fighting for their legitimate rights and against the aggression and repression of international imperialism.

OMA has been honoured by the presence in our country of friendly delegations, within the framework of solidarity and reciprocity between peoples and their women's organizations. We have had visits by women's organizations, most of them led by their presidents, in particular from Zambia, the People's Republic of Congo, the Pan-African Women's Organization, the Soviet Union, Czechoslovakia, Bulgaria, Cuba, Sweden, Mozambique, Guinea Bissau, Cape Verde and São Tomé. Those visits have permitted an exchange of views and the consolidation of the bonds of friendship between OMA and other women's organizations. We should make special mention of the honour of the visit by the first woman cosmonaut, Valentina Tereshkova Nikolayeva, President of the Soviet Women's Committee.

OMA has received gifts from women's organizations and other bodies to help the Angolans who have been victims of racist South Africa's aggression, in particular from:

— Soviet Women's Committee
— Czech Union of Women
— Union of Democratic German Women (GDR)
— Bulgarian Women's Committee
— Democratic Women's Movement (Portugal)
— Organization of Women of Cape Verde
— Women's Union for Peace and Progress (Basel, Switzerland)
— Hungarian Women's Council
— A group of Swedish women
— ICCO
— United Nations Development Programme (UNDP)
— United Nations.Children's Fund (UNICEF)
— SIDA (Sweden)

On behalf of the population which has benefited from this humanitarian aid, we here wish to express our profound gratitude.

We take this opportunity to express sincere wishes for the continuity and strengthening of the bonds that have now for many years governed relations between OMA and organizations the world over which share our ideals of peace, justice and social progress.

The Position of Angolan Women Today

1. Ideology

As already stated, the First Congress of the MPLA described OMA as 'the organization of all Angolan women fighting for their emancipation and their complete engagement in the tasks of the revolution and socialist construction'. The struggle for the emancipation of women and their engagement in the tasks of the revolution demands of OMA intensive mobilizing and organizing work and, more especially, political and ideological education to enable women to understand their important role in life and society.

In order to carry out the task of political education and heightening the consciousness of Angolan women, OMA has trained 103 political cadres at home and abroad, and 67 activists who, in neighbourhoods, communes and municipalities, encourage and mobilize women to join the Organization. These political cadres and activists explain to the population, and especially to women, the main guidelines of the Party and the objectives of OMA. At the same time, they sound out the problems and concerns of the masses of the people, in order to pass them on to leading bodies.

With a view to heightening women's love for their country and the revolution, OMA has organized talks, seminars and combatants' bonfire gatherings in all the provinces. On the occasion of the commemoration of important historical dates, voluntary labour campaigns are organized in which thousands of women take part throughout the country.

2. Education

Education has always been a major concern of our Organization. From the very earliest days of its existence, it devoted itself to literacy teaching and raising the educational and professional level of women. Indeed, we were aware from the very outset that without education and vocational and technical training there could be no emancipation or liberation for women.

The educational and profoundly humanist value of the Organization's work in the field of literacy teaching was internationally recognized, and in 1973, at the proposal of the WIDF, Unesco awarded OMA the Nadejda Krupskaya Literacy Prize. The great political significance of this Unesco decision should be stressed, because it was a way of recognizing the efforts made in literacy work by fighting women.

Our Organization continues to play a very active part in literacy campaigns organized by the National Literacy Centre, by mobilizing and encouraging women to study and by providing literacy teachers and primary teachers. Study circles have been set up in all provinces to facilitate literacy teaching within OMA.

In October 1982, of the 673,968 people who had become literate, 288,168 (about 42.7%) were women. Of this total, 13,257 were women in the defence and security forces, 29,418 women workers, 144,367 peasant women and 101,126 unspecified working women and housewives. Among the women who completed literacy courses were a number of OMA officials.

With a view to providing Angolan women, especially in the rural areas, with basic education to enable them to solve some of the fundamental problems of our society, the Huambo Vocational Training Centre was set up with the collaboration of the UNDP. Subjects taught at the Centre are Portuguese, agriculture, health and hygiene, literacy, social and natural science, and political education. After completing the course, women return to their places of origin to apply their general knowledge in their community and, after that period of practical work, return to pursue their studies at the Centre. The second course for development promoters is now under way, attended by women students from every province in the country.

OMA is not at present involved in any action regarding the choice of courses for women students at intermediate or university level. Up to October 1982, it was found that most of the women in higher education were in the faculties of medicine and economics. Of a total of 217 who have graduated, 72 are women, which is about 33.1%.

3. Productive and Social Work

In our country work is a source of honour. Work dignifies human beings and is a pre-condition for their developm. nt. Interpreting this principle, OMA promotes the emancipation of women, encouraging them to participate in socially useful work.

Statistical data on the participation of women in productive work reveal the effort still required, because the percentage of women employed in various fields of activity is around 20%. This is a relatively low percentage if we consider that women are about half the country's active population. One of the main reasons for this is the high rate of illiteracy and the low general education of women.

It should not, however, be forgotten that women's work is predominantly agricultural and that agriculture has been defined as the base of our development. Agricultural enterprises, especially those related to coffee, comprise hundreds of women, although not all of them work on a permanent basis. Women in the countryside are mainly engaged in subsistence agriculture, and the serious problems the country is experiencing make their lives even more difficult. In roughly built homes scattered throughout the countryside, using the most rudimentary implements, ignorant of the most elementary rules for protecting their own health or that of their families, their lives are guided by sunrise and sunset. Their work is the repetitious tilling of fields whose meagre produce is either consumed by the family or bartered for other goods which are immediately consumed.

The twofold task women have when engaged in socially useful work makes it extremely difficult for them to involve themselves in the country's social, political and economic life. Traditionally relegated to working in the fields and looking after their homes and children, Angolan women are awakening to a new life and a new concept of being in the world. With a view to easing the twofold task that falls upon women when they engage in productive work, our Government has opened a number of establishments to care for children during the hours when their mothers are working. The First Meeting of Working Mothers promoted by our Organization, in September 1978, echoed women's concern about this matter, noting that it was not possible to go out to work unless there was someone to look after the children.

The meeting was a great success because it permitted close contact and frank discussion between women from all the country's provinces who face similar problems and share the same goals. The First Meeting of Working Mothers recommended that measures be taken in the field of mother-and-child care, creating minimum conditions for running creches and canteens at workplaces. This event marked a new phase in the activity

of women workers in a number of enterprises who promoted
the setting up of creches, nurseries and child care centres.
In 1982 meetings of working mothers were held in all provinces,
at which women concluded that the resolutions of the first
meeting had to a great extent remained unfulfilled, and once
again stressed the urgent need to create conditions that
would enable women to engage in socially useful work.
Creating public laundries and school canteens, opening more
child care centres and creches, providing drinking water wells
and channelling drinking water to rural areas are some of the
concerns recorded by OMA which it will with energy and
persistence take up with the appropriate bodies.

The provincial meetings of working mothers have drawn
women's attention to the unstable nature of women's labour
in our country. The General Labour Law, which represents
a victory for Angolan women, cannot be applied in respect
of women who, through their lack of consciousness and sense
of responsibility, jeopardize production by staying at home.
The law is to protect working women and not those who take
up productive work merely in order to earn wages, and then
stay at home allegedly in accordance with the clauses of that
law. Those meetings have been a rich experience for our
Organization, and OMA must struggle to ensure the implementation of the resolutions adopted and redouble its efforts
to raise the consciousness of working women.

Our Organization's work in the field of productive labour
in all provinces has centred mainly on women workers in
the textile industry and on women agricultural workers in
state enterprises, co-operatives and collective farms. Days of
voluntary work in harvesting coffee, cotton and groundnuts
are one activity that has mobilized hundreds of women in the
different provinces.

OMA has taken part in other campaigns such as the cleaning
and embellishment of towns and villages. In some provinces
OMA's sewing centres have helped to instil the idea that
practical and useful work can ensure women's participation
and at the same time give them a few notions which are
useful in their everyday life. OMA will increasingly encourage
women to contribute to national reconstruction by taking
part in socially useful work, because it regards this as the
basic pre-condition for true emancipation.

As regards the social work done after independence, when

health and education were provided free of charge, OMA has
started to work closely with the government bodies
concerned, particularly with the Ministry of Health, the
Ministry of Education and the State Secretariat for Social
Affairs.

Our activity in the field of health has been directed
essentially towards recruiting cadres, taking part in vaccination campaigns and visiting hospitals, presenting the patients
with gifts and holding talks. At the national level, OMA has
trained 184 health promoters, 40 health defenders, 287
traditional midwives and 4 assistant midwives. We have taken
part in the administering of 1,265,937 anti-polio vaccines and
280,895 vaccines against other diseases. Support given to
patients and health workers has included 1,249 visits to
hospitals, 616 talks, and the opening of 19 health centres
at which 126,789 pregnant women have received care. The
special attention given to health stems from the fact that
there are a large number of women (9,686) working in that
sector — 4,235 in Luanda, 776 in Huambo and 72 in Cunene,
for example.

As regards social welfare, OMA has made a significant
contribution to the solution of problems that have arisen
especially with the return of compatriots who have lived
abroad, the displacement of thousands of persons as a result
of racist South Africa's aggression against our country, and
the many war widows and orphans who need our support.
OMA has contributed to the support of 888 war widows,
13,013 war orphans and 40,674 displaced persons, and has
also raised funds and provided support for the institutions
responsible for dealing with those problems. During this
period, OMA has opened 5 creches in the provinces of
Luanda, Huambo, Namibe (formerly Moçâmedes) and
Huíla, encouraged the opening of 4 creches at workplaces,
trained 72 child care assistants and made 1,249 visits to
help the aged.

Special mention should be made of OMA's participation
in the International Year of the Child, the National Commission of which was headed by OMA's National Co-ordinator.
In the course of 1979, the National Commission, through
its various sub-commissions, studied the problems of childhood and infancy, organized a number of political, cultural
and social events, and drew up a programme of future

initiatives to discuss the situation of children in our country.

In view of the population's huge social problems resulting from difficulties with supplies, medical care, transport and housing, OMA has promoted action aimed at implementing the decisions of the meetings of working mothers.

4. Information and Propaganda

Tempered by the experience gained during the national liberation struggle, after independence OMA defined information and propaganda work as an essential aspect of women's emancipation, aimed at informing the entire population of its activities in various spheres of national life.

A number of propaganda programmes have been drawn up, based on the Party's directives, while others have been prepared as work plans and sent to the provinces for implementation, especially those related to support for the various campaigns OMA promotes and takes part in.

The 2 and 8 March are dates to which the OMA has always paid special attention. Various political and cultural activities have been organized to ensure that those days are properly commemorated. Similarly, 9 August, South African Women's Day, has been a day of solidarity with the South African women and people and with all fighting peoples in the world. African Women's Day, 31 July, is also a date on which we organize the same kind of activities. National and international commemorative days have been emphasized in such a way as to help heighten the patriotism and sense of solidarity of women and the people as a whole.

The UN Decade for Women involved a special programme of work. OMA promoted it by publicizing its objectives through talks, round-table conferences and meetings, many of them attended by officials of the MPLA-Workers' Party.

In order to publicize the objectives of the World Congress of Women, held in October 1981 in the Socialist Republic of Czechoslovakia, OMA prepared written material issued to the mass media and graphic propaganda distributed throughout the country.

Since it was initially announced, the First OMA Congress has made a special propaganda effort to publicize the theses and all the preparatory work. There has been good collaboration with the information media, especially with the National

Radio, which has very closely followed the Congress's work. Apart from informative propaganda, graphic work has included T-shirts, calendars, booklets, posters, badges and so forth. In this respect, we should like to stress the support we have received from EDIL.

As regards written propaganda, in addition to OMA's official bulletin, which has a print run of more than 20,000, a Special Bulletin has been issued entirely dedicated to the OMA Congress. We regret the present lack of bulletins in English and French, mainly owing to the shortage of cadres.

In fulfilment of a resolution of the Fourth Congress of the Pan-African Women's Organization, and with the support of the MPLA-Workers' Party, a Regional Centre for Southern Africa and an Information Centre of the Pan-African Women's Organization in support of the national liberation movements have been set up. The activities carried out by those centres have included seminars and talks for women peasants and workers in Huambo and Lunda Sul Provinces, to inform them of the struggle and the lives of Namibian and South African women. Photographic exhibitions, film shows and meetings have also been held for the same purpose. Although there are plans for a periodical on the activities of the centres, it has not yet come into being.

Another highly important activity promoted by OMA has been organizing marches to protest against South African aggression against our country, bringing together not only women but men and children.

Internationally, activities had been programmed to publicize the work of the Pan-African Women's Information Centre in some African countries, although this was not done for various reasons. However, OMA took part in the proceedings of the seminar organized by the WIDF on the influence of the mass media on women, the family and children, which was held in Panama. There we denounced the terrorist South African operations in the southern part of our continent and their harmful effects on our women and children.

5. Financial Activity
Financial activity is known to be a key factor, for the existence of funds favours and furthers the political and ideological work of any organization. OMA's financial resources, although not sufficient for the growing expenditure it faces,

have shown some improvement. We must not forget, however, that a substantial part of OMA's expenditure has been met by funds granted by the Party. Clearly most of our expenditure goes to pay salaries, to carry out tasks entrusted to OMA's Department of Information and Propaganda, to buy petrol for our vehicles and to fund banking transactions when our delegations go abroad. Salaries are paid on a national basis, covering the provinces and their various municipalities.

As regards the question of the payment of dues by OMA members, it must be acknowledged that there are still some failings under the present system. More work to heighten consciousness is needed to ensure the payment of dues. Once this is achieved, dues can be included as one of the limited sources from which OMA acquires its funds. Speaking of dues, we should also include the sale of articles of various descriptions (clothing, textiles, etc.) as one of the principal methods of raising funds.

Up to now, income and expenditure have balanced out; so we have a positive balance.

In the colonial period, the problem of the involvement of Angolan women in the development process could not be dissociated from the ways in which African labour as a whole was exploited. The position of women reflected all modern problems of urbanization and industrialization, as well as those of the traditional way of life based on the exploitation of domestic work. In the process of capitalist development, the position of women was affected by all the problems which men experienced at first hand — unemployment, the lack of social advancement, economic over-exploitation, racism, alcoholism, and so forth.

Oppressed as they were by a social order which exploited them, men found in women a great outlet for venting and avenging their own dissatisfaction. This took forms such as the exploitation of domestic work, prostitution, the dowry system and sheer contempt. Since there were no overall solutions to the problems, many women dared to face up to them through their own individual initiative, finding dignity, stability and social advancement through work. But the majority of women survived only with difficulties which sometimes led them into prostitution.

With our country's independence, conditions were created

to achieve the emancipation of women by involving them in productive work on an equal footing with men, as ensured by the General Labour Law of the People's Republic of Angola.

In rural areas, women now take part in decision-making to solve their problems and those of the community. Indeed, 250,000 women are members of peasant associations, gaining experience in collective work, taking part in literacy classes and learning to use agricultural machinery. The number of women members of agricultural co-operatives is 35,000. They have left behind traditional forms of agriculture to discover the advantages of collective work.

In rural and peripheral areas, 50,747 women are working in state enterprises concerned with agricultural and livestock production and coffee. In towns, too, the pace of life has taken 80,000 women away from their homes and invisible work. They are now contributing to national reconstruction and their own social advancement in transport, construction, education, light and heavy industry, health, administrative work, public services, the food industry, fisheries and information.

Women are represented in Party and State organs. There are four women members on the Central Committee of our Party, the MPLA-Workers' Party; 17 are members of the highest organ of State power, the People's Assembly, and there is one woman member of the Government. Also to be considered are the hundreds of women workers in the various sectors of our economy who are departmental heads, local women Party and State leaders, women deputies at provincial level, of whom there are about 100, and women municipal and communal commissioners, who are already a stimulus to others to engage in productive work and to take decisions of collective importance.

As already mentioned, it has been OMA's constant concern to galvanize the full initiative of Angolan women, and at the same time provide them with facilities and opportunities to prepare themselves professionally to assume the responsibilities required in various sectors and to acquire the political and ideological education demanded by the revolution.

In choosing the theme of this Congress — 'Unity, Organization, Development' — we wished to revive the flame of the great tradition of struggle of our people, and of Angolan women in particular, in seeking overall solutions within the framework of the process of building socialism, to transform

the mentality of men and women alike, so as to ensure
effective equality, in a better future for our main human
resource: the children of today. Among the overall solutions
were priorities such as the creation of mechanisms to
guarantee effective participation of women and the social
legitimacy of institutions dealing particularly with women's
problems.

In industry and public services, where women are socially
equal with men, it is necessary to ensure recognition of the
special work and social problems affecting women, bearing in
mind the barriers to be overcome not only because of interests
alien to the position of women, but also because of the attitude
of women themselves, who constitute a highly heterogeneous
grouping with differing interests which are not always easily
reconciled.

In view of this situation, OMA proposes to establish forms
of organization which will help to release the immense force
of women (already shown by the perseverance, resignation
and selflessness of mothers, wives and daughters) and to
channel it into creative activity, and also to help ensure
recognition of women's value as human beings.

The Problems Still Facing Women Are Many and Varied

As we have just said, the problems still faced by Angolan
women are many and varied. Some of those problems are a
direct consequence of the situation in our country, underdeveloped and under daily attack by imperialism which
wants to deny us the right to be free, sovereign and independent, and to show our solidarity with all oppressed peoples.

OMA and all Angolan women must be united and organized
in the struggle for peace and development, against the South
African racists and the Angolan puppets, lackeys of imperialism, because we know that without peace and development
we shall never achieve total emancipation for women in our
country. That is why our involvement in the tasks of defending
our national territory and the tasks of production is an
integral and fundamental part of our struggle for emancipation.

There are other problems that women experience in their
everyday lives which are a result not of external factors but
of objective and subjective internal factors. It is up to

us to give impetus to their solution, because we experience and feel them more intensely. And it is in this sphere that our Organization must make the greatest efforts, so that women may be involved and participate ever more actively in all aspects of national life, exercising their full rights.

Over the coming years, therefore, OMA must make serious efforts in organizing and running its work, so as substantially to improve that work. And in the discussions we have during this Congress and the principles we establish, OMA's leadership will find the basis and the strength to be ever more active and effective in carrying out its tasks, so as to respond promptly to the requirements of Angolan women and efficiently to play the part which, as a mass organization, falls to it in building socialism in our country.

We must be an instrument for sounding out the anxieties and concerns of Angolan women and, together with the appropriate structures, we must ensure that solutions are found.

OMA's Aims and Tasks

The aims of our activity in the coming period will be the following:

1. Significantly to increase the Organization's membership and to make members take an active part in matters related to OMA's internal life.
2. To give fresh impetus to creating conditions to combat illiteracy and raise the educational, vocational, technical and scientific level of women, and to encourage the development of their artistic abilities.
3. To contribute to the ever more active participation of Angolan women in all sectors of national life, in defence and security bodies, enterprises, co-operatives and public services, so that women may constitute an example of our capacity for struggle and resistance against imperialism and the puppets.
4. To give fresh impetus to political and ideological work among women, on the basis of the guidelines of the MPLA-Workers' Party, so that women may understand the transformations underway in our country and their own

role in the revolution.

5. To dignify and significantly improve the living and working conditions of peasant women, creating conditions to increase their knowledge, schooling and vocational and technical training.

In order to achieve these objectives we shall have to do a great deal of work over the coming years in organization, political, technical and vocational education, production, social work, information and propaganda, and in all other fields in which we are capable of contributing to women's true emancipation and to the advance of the revolution.

Organizational Work

In the sphere of organization, OMA must improve its working methods at every level through a better application of the principles of democratic centralism. This calls for annual plans based on the ideas and initiatives of the branches, bearing in mind the tasks and guidelines laid down by leading Party structures and State bodies. Once they are approved, these plans will be the basis for our activity. The work done will be periodically assessed and new tasks will be set for the ensuing period.

This work will be supported by visits from members of leading organs to assist and supervise the work of structures at lower levels. If these principles are to be properly applied, it is imperative that statistical information be improved and the documentation and information centre organized.

In the recruitment of new members, it is important to give impetus to the work of activists and branches, so that each new member may feel properly guided and have tasks to fulfil.

Finally, in order to improve organizational work, the National Committee to be elected must in the coming months regulate questions related to the composition and specific attributes of the National Executive Secretariat and provincial, municipal and communal secretariats, the number of members of provincial, municipal and communal committees and the structuring and running of branch secretariats.

With regard to finance, matters related to the payment of dues will have to be improved, through better organization and intensive political work. We shall also ensure improvements in the drawing up of the annual budget and supervision of its use.

Education
A special effort must be made in education, so as to raise the
cultural, technical and political level of Angolan women, as
an indispensable pre-condition for the advance of the
revolution. In the field of literacy, a priority task, there is a
need to study ways of achieving greater participation by
women, and, if need be, to further it through the use of moral
and material incentives.

Constantly to increase the political, ideological and
educational training of OMA cadres, at every level, and that of
all who work in the Organization, is an indispensable aspect
of improving our work.

We have to find ways for branches to work actively in the
following fields:

— Raising the educational level of housewives.
— Supporting schools, especially by providing teachers and
  promoting extra-curricular activities.
— Starting courses in dressmaking, cooking, gardening and
  so forth, in which political education, literacy and health
  matters can be included.
— Starting adult evening classes in rural areas, particularly
  for peasants, with short courses in which women from the
  countryside can study a number of useful subjects.

OMA will work on these matters in close collaboration with
the appropriate Party and State structures, in order to
achieve more positive results through combined effort.

Political and ideological education, the aim of which is
to explain to women the scientific theories of the evolution
of society in order to enable them to understand the reasons
for the difficulties we now face and to overcome them, will
be an essential means of fighting the ills and vices inherited
from colonialism. Simple and practical study material must be
prepared and effective ways sought to hold study circles
specially for women.

OMA will continue to promote literacy work and raise the
educational, technical and scientific level of women. Our aim
will be to make women aware of the fact that much more is
demanded of them than of men, so that if they do not know

how to read and write and have not had proper vocational and technical training, they will be able to work only in a subordinate capacity, as unskilled workers.

Our women need to study, to be encouraged to follow courses through which they can fully develop; and they require conditions that will lead to the habit of reading, practising sport and freely developing their artistic abilities.

Defence of the Country
OMA reaffirms to the bodies responsible for national defence the readiness of all Angolan women fully to participate in all tasks required in the defence of our territorial integrity and of the gains already made.

In the People's Armed Forces for the Liberation of Angola (FAPLA), in the People's Defence Organization (ODP), in fields and factories, we are prepared to lay down our lives to ensure the defeat of the enemy and a free and happy future. We shall support our combatants in every way necessary. We shall support their families and households so that the honourable task of defending the country is shared by all.

The Social Field
In the social field OMA will work towards:

— Helping to explain the duties and obligations arising from jobs relating to the public, such as health and public services.
— Helping to educate and mobilize women for the tasks of cleansing, ensuring hygiene and embellishing houses in the neighbourhoods and towns.
— Helping to combat delinquency and anti-social practices, especially on the part of women.
— Supporting health programmes.
— Supporting creches and children's homes.

Children's problems and assistance for orphans and juvenile delinquents will receive our full attention, and it is up to us to propose the requisite measures and tasks to the bodies concerned.

OMA will thus be able to make life in our towns and villages healthier and more beautiful, relations between citizens in our country more harmonious and our people happier.

Our Congress theses and OMA's participation in the recent workshop on the situation of children allow us to conclude that action on behalf of children should be carried out in three fields:

— Pre-natal care.
— Mother-and-child care.
— Care for children with special problems.

Pre-Natal Care
Pregnancy should be a result of the couple's conscious decision, which implies that both have already acquired the physiological, psychological and social maturity needed to enable the pregnancy to develop under the best possible conditions for both mother and child. Hence the need for OMA to take an active part in five kinds of activity:

(i) Sex Education for Young People: Sex takes place at ages when the maturity referred to above has not yet been acquired, and it is therefore most important that young people should be sufficiently well informed of all the problems caused by a possible accidental pregnancy. At the same time, unfortunately adults often take advantage of that immaturity and exploit especially girls sexually. The sex education of young people should therefore be accompanied by the education of the community as a whole, making it possible to detect and punish any such abuses.

(ii) Spacing of Pregnancies: Present knowledge shows that it is essential to the health of mother and children that one pregnancy should follow another after a period of no less than two years. This implies at the same time correct and constant information on the serious risk of 'permanent pregnancy' and the setting up of centres easily accessible to the country's entire population where, in addition to such information, there are scientific means which make it possible to prevent pregnancy.

A further conclusion is that it is also necessary to organize services in places which have the minimum requisite conditions to terminate an unwanted pregnancy.

Impetus will be given to the running of local meeting centres where women can study and discuss the problems they face. The purpose is to create conditions at these centres for women to receive guidance in legal, economic, social and other spheres.

Impetus will also be given to the preparation of studies on a number of themes related to women — the position of women in our country; the part they have played in our history, especially during the national liberation struggle; the position of women in Africa; in short, research that will enable us to know and to honour our heroines better, and to help us solve our problems more adequately.

In social work, OMA's activity will be directed towards two essential goals: on the one hand, that of educating women so as to enable them to carry out their countless tasks more effectively; and, on the other, that of contributing to the solution of the social problems our country faces. With regard to the former aspect, OMA will have an important role to play, especially in the following spheres.

OMA will work to make women aware of their role in the family and of the principles on which it should be based: equality between men and women in the family and in every field, especially in respect of marriage, the education of children, supporting the family and doing domestic work. New legislation to this effect is urgently needed.

The education of children assumes special importance in this phase, since it is necessary to teach them to respect their country and the revolution and to be internationalists; to show respect for older people and to be polite to women, so that they may become the builders of a socialist society.

OMA will take a number of initiatives in the sphere of health education for women, in towns and more especially in rural areas, so that women may themselves solve some of the health problems they face.

By means of public health courses and guided debates, the setting up of health brigades, cleansing and embellishment campaigns, and by promoting the use of traditional medicine, OMA will spread among women the knowledge they need in order to prevent disease. In this respect, sex education and family planning assume special importance, since they are closely related to women's health and to family equilibrium. In co-operation with the Ministry of Health, OMA will carry out explanatory work on the objectives of family planning.

(iii) Establishing a Minimum Age of Consent: In view of what
has been said above, it would be important to give the force
of law to a minimum age for pregnancy. Sex education for
young people and the population as a whole, together with the
establishment throughout the country of centres providing
for the proper use of contraceptive methods, would make it
possible for provincial people's assemblies to carry out a
careful study of a future law defining the minimum age for
pregnancy.

(iv) Support for Pregnant Workers: Although the General
Labour Law establishes the rights of pregnant women in
enterprises, there is as yet no legal protection for rural
workers or housewives. OMA could promote, together with
the Ministry of Agriculture and the mass media, a study of
the various mechanisms which would make it possible to
organize more efficient assistance for pregnant rural workers
and housewives. Peasant associations and co-operatives, the
family, the village and the neighbourhood should be the
sites and the subject of such a study, so as to ensure that
pregnant women have the essential care their condition
requires.

(v) The Right to Essential Nutrition: One of the basic factors
in a successful pregnancy is that provision be made for
essential nutritional requirements. Meeting these requirements
should be a right, and OMA will therefore have the extremely
important role of promoting an entire process which will
include supplies of food supplements, a study of local
possibilities of improving nutrition and educating the family
in order that they may understand the importance of proper
nutrition during pregnancy.

Mother-and-Child Care
In the first year: It has been fully established that it is
essential to the harmonious development of the new-born
child that he or she remains in close contact with the mother
for the first 12 months. Not only should mothers have
facilities for breast-feeding during that period, but one should
also allow for every form of maternal warmth so important

117

to the child's psychological development. It is therefore up to OMA constantly to stress, in labour bodies and the mass media, in families and neighbourhoods, the need to maintain the mother-child bond until such time as the child takes its first steps.

Up to the first year of schooling: During this period the child moves about in the family circle and in the neighbourhood. Children's playgrounds are therefore needed. OMA can promote two main activities: mobilization in the neighbourhoods with a view to the provision of the necessary equipment for children and of facilities for watching over, maintaining and improving that equipment, and participation in the running of children's playgrounds.

Essential nutrition: Breast-fed babies, babies that are being weaned and those in the subsequent phases of infant development also have essential nutritional requirements. What has already been said about the period of pregnancy also applies to those phases.

Care for Children with Special Problems
Orphans, abandoned and displaced children, and children with special problems which partially incapacitate them, form a large group which has unfortunately been increasing in number. OMA can help to make executive structures and the population as a whole aware of these problems, applying itself to listing, classifying and locating such children; promoting and taking part in the study and organization of programmes to deal with the very grave situation of such children; and starting immediate action to provide short-term help as far as we can with our present limited possibilities.

Production will be one of the most effective means of mobilizing women. It is no exaggeration to say that Angolan women are the country's major producers. We are referring to the peasant women who produce the greater part of the country's agricultural wealth in their fields, and now also in production co-operatives.

We find a different situation in towns, where many women neither study nor work and are therefore economically and socially very dependent. Women's involvement in work in urban areas is therefore a fundamental task. At the same time, campaigns need to be promoted against absenteeism and for increased production and productivity. Particularly important in this respect are voluntary labour campaigns which, when well organized, contribute significantly to the mobilization and education of women.

Women's technical and vocational skills need to be promoted, so as to make it easier for women like housewives, for those who stop working for personal reasons and for newly literate women, to have a socially useful occupation. It should not, however, be forgotten that the question of women and labour is closely bound up with the establishment of conditions which enable them to free themselves from the heavy burden of domestic work and bringing up children.

The various meetings of working mothers held throughout the country reached similar conclusions on the following needs:

— More and better creches.
— Opening collective laundries.
— Setting up canteens in schools and workplaces, and industrial kitchens.
— Improving supplies of essential goods in the country and combating speculation and hoarding.
— Improving transport facilities.
— Setting up mills in agricultural co-operatives.

In this respect, priority should be given to social support for working mothers to minimize their family tasks.

In the field of information, a great effort must be made to publicize among all our people the tasks we are carrying out at various levels of our Organization, our problems, our difficulties and the successes we are going to score. We shall have to launch far-reaching agitation and mobilization campaigns to publicize our objectives and the means of attaining them. We need to give special publicity to examples of women workers whose work in the various fields of political, economic, social and cultural life has been especially outstanding.

In the field of external relations, our Organization will continue to establish and develop friendly relations and co-operation with women's organizations, women's sections of political parties and women personalities, with special emphasis on those from our continent's liberation movements and from African and socialist countries. We shall continue

to show solidarity with the women and peoples of the world
who are fighting for freedom, independence and social
progress. And those contacts will be one of the ways of
publicizing abroad the successes of the Angolan revolution
and the important role played by women in scoring those
successes.

It is with sincere joy that we welcome among us today the
friendly presence of one of the founders of our Organization,
without wishing to hurt the feelings of anyone present or
absent — and we do not include among the latter those who
have gone forever but still live on in our hearts. Let me introduce those who are in this hall.

To these comrades and friends and to all the old militants
who were in the MPLA's First, Second, Third, Fourth and
Fifth Politico-Military Regions, as well as to those who took
part in clandestine OMA activities, we express our deepest
thanks for the work done, which has today borne fruit. To
all of them the First OMA Congress expresses a special greeting.

On this occasion we reaffirm our unshakeable solidarity
with the brother peoples of Namibia, South Africa, the
Sahrawi Arab Democratic Republic, East Timor and Palestine
who, led by their vanguard parties, are heroically fighting
for their right to happiness, peace and progress. We also
extend our solidarity to the peoples of Nicaragua, El Salvador
and other countries in Latin America fighting for the consolidation of national independence or against fascist regimes
in US pay, as well as to the peoples of the Persian Gulf, the
Indian Ocean and the Red Sea, who want to make their
regions zones of peace, demanding the dismantling of military
bases on their territory; to the peoples of Asia who face
external threats from imperialism, and to the peoples of
European countries who, because of the aggressive policy
of the imperialist forces, see their sovereignty and peace
threatened by a nuclear war with catastrophic consequences.

The work of our Organization has been carried out in the
face of difficulties of every kind, both material and human,
as was to be expected in a young country which faces a
politico-military situation that prevents its full development.

In presenting this report, we seek above all to reflect the
spirit of militancy and dedication which has guided us in the

course of the long life of our Organization.

The resolutions that come out of this Congress should be implemented with the greatest enthusiasm, in the certainty that this task will be a big step forward in the advance of the revolution.

For the Emancipation of Women
The Struggle Continues!
Victory is Certain!

6. Closing Speech by Lucio Lara, MPLA-Workers Party Central Committee Secretary for Organization

It is with great satisfaction and great expectations that our people, the militants of the MPLA-Workers' Party and, above all, the women of Angola have been following the various phases of this very important OMA Congress, now ending after six days during which its proceedings have had an intensive impact.

After the preparatory work culminating in the holding of provincial assemblies and the election of their leading bodies, the best possible portent for the success of this Congress was the fact that it was opened by the country's leader, Comrade President José Eduardo dos Santos, who put forward far-reaching guidelines, placing in their true context the issues raised by OMA in the thesis submitted to the Congress, thereby enriching the debates and final resolutions. That was the Party's greatest contribution to this Congress, which during the preparatory phases also had the constant support of the Party's various organs, the Party Youth and other sectors of national life.

Women Must Be Politically Organized

It should be stressed that in referring to the new prospects opened for work among the masses, and especially among women, owing to the conditions under which we are waging the struggle for national reconstruction and socialism, Comrade President described as 'a great challenge to our ability and intelligence' the need to use 'all present possibilities to ensure that women are politically organized and cultivated for the tasks of OMA, national reconstruction and our country's defence'. Referring to the need for the decisive 'step forward' that everyone expects of OMA, he described as 'the great target to be attained' that of educating, mobilizing and organizing the largest possible number of women'. The Congress accepted the challenge with enthusiasm.

The courageous issues contained in the various theses dealing with a long list of burning problems which have hindered Angolan women's struggle for emancipation have now become Congress resolutions which will henceforth guide all OMA's action programmes in different fields of activity. The important resolutions adopted, based on the theses discussed, are imbued with wise realism and are in keeping with the deepest aspirations of women, as shown by the applause that greeted the resolution on Women and the Family.

The great gains already achieved by Angolan women during the liberation struggle have since national independence been added to by further gains which cannot, of course, be dissociated from the process of building the socialist society we are planning. Its foundations are being laid under violent conditions of war, starting off with small-scale production with a very poor output, a seriously unbalanced economy and very difficult living conditions for the people, entailing great sacrifices and worry for women. This is why the Congress has emphasized women's attitude to the war and to production, as regards their active involvement, whether in defence and security bodies or in the tasks of production and organizing resistance in every sector, both in the countryside and in towns.

Recent meetings of the MPLA-Workers' Party Central Committee and the People's Assembly took extremely important decisions on dealing with the critical situation the country faces, both as regards the war and in the economic and financial sphere. The measures advocated, prompted by the need to establish habits of austerity, hard work, national saving and increased production, particularly food production, are part of a series of emergency programmes whose implementation involves not only workers in the sectors concerned, but also the Party, the Party Youth, the Government and mass organizations, especially OMA, whose role in mass mobilization and participation assumes great importance.

Your presence at these proceedings, representing more than a million OMA members, is of decisive importance at this time, since you have the responsibility of instilling awareness in all Angolan women, and giving them, as well as your partners, husbands, sons, fathers and brothers, an impetus in the great effort required of our people, who are at war.

We all recall the unshakeable confidence placed by the late Comrade President António Agostinho Neto in the mobilizing capacity of women and the caring way in which he orientated OMA in the decisive activity it was called upon to undertake during the national liberation struggle and, after independence, in the tasks of national reconstruction. To this day, in its activity among the masses of the people, OMA continues to draw inspiration from the teachings of the late Immortal Guide.

We have seen the enthusiasm with which the theses on the Emancipation of Women, Working Women and Women and the Family have been debated. For the first time it has been possible for you Angolan women, as an important sector of our society, jointly to assess a number of problems directly affecting you which have never before been raised in a systematic way.

More Just Conditions in Our Society

The Party and the State are now in possession of valuable elements which will make it possible to programme action to solve many of the problems facing our women both in the countryside and in towns. This will help to establish more just conditions in our society. Correcting some anachronistic laws and combating certain phenomena affecting young women, working mothers, women at home, pregnant women and children have now become immediate courses of action for Party and Government bodies.

The need for greater support for the training of women cadres and for cautious but decisive action in respect of mothers and children, as well as the serious nutritional and educational problems in this field, demanding the participation of the whole community, have already prompted some action programmes. Their fulfilment will require the active participation of OMA, now better armed with the conclusions of its Congress.

We believe that when you enthusiastically adopted the various resolutions which will guide you in your irresistible advance to effective equal rights you were not thinking of that alone. You were also thinking of the difficulties you face in running your homes, with the rising cost of living. You were thinking of the occupied part of Cunene Province, of the battlefronts where your sons, husbands and brothers daily face the murderous weapons of the racist South African troops and their puppets manipulated by imperialism who, supported by the Reagan administration, have once again launched their war machine against Angola and are extending their destabilization strategy to the whole of Southern Africa.

OMA, in co-operation with the appropriate Party and Government bodies, has an important role to play in the fight against the high cost of living, by uncovering black-marketeeing networks, helping to improve supplies and production and joining the future People's Vigilance Brigades.

While making gigantic efforts to increase FAPLA's defensive capability, our Party and Government have made unstinting efforts to find peaceful ways of solving problems, whether through the UN, talks with the so-called Contact Group in conjunction with the Frontline States, or bilateral talks with the aggressors. The principles guiding our attitude in this situation of a war created by South Africa — which is illegally occupying Namibia and part of our territory — have won the approval of all African and Non-Aligned countries, socialist countries and almost all UN member states. Our support for the liberation struggle of the Namibian people, through SWAPO, is in accordance with the principles enshrined in the UN Charter and UN resolutions, as well as with the internationalist practice of our Party, which remains unalterable.

It was in the context of that internationalist practice that, at our request at the time of the 1975 invasions, friendly Cuban forces came to our aid. Their presence has been the subject of speculation by reactionary imperialist circles who are attempting blackmail by demanding their withdrawal as a pre-condition for a Namibian settlement. That blackmail has also been rejected by African countries, socialist countries

and the majority of UN member states which have fully
understood the meaning of the joint Angolan-Cuban statement of 4 February 1982. That imperialist policy of blackmail will once again be repudiated at the summit meeting
of Non-Aligned states which has just opened in New Delhi.

The Solidarity of Women the World Over

During these days solidarity with our people has been
reinvigorated and enriched by the warm solidarity which
friendly delegations from the whole world have brought our
women at their Congress.

Here the fighting sisters of what was the CONCP have
again met, and also the democratic women of Portugal, who
have always extended their friendship to our people and to
their Party.

Here we have heard expressed the warm solidarity of
women from many African countries, particularly from
countries with which we share borders.

Here we have the organized women from socialist countries,
our allies, who have reaffirmed their long-standing support for
OMA.

Here there are women's organizations of liberation movements from every continent who, arms in hand, are pursuing
with determination their victorious liberation struggle against
retrograde forces.

Here there are friendly delegations from organizations in
Europe, Latin America and Asia, as well as from the WIDF,
the Afro-Asian People's Organization and the Pan-African
Women's Organization. All of them recall with friendship
our Immortal Guide Comrade President Agostinho Neto.

All of them have condemned the permanent aggression to
which we are subjected by South Africa. All have warmly
expressed their unconditional support for OMA and the
Angolan people. All have helped to enrich the Congress with
their experience in organizing or participating in national
development.

Through them it has been possible to recall illustrious
heroes and heroines of Africa, Asia, Europe and Latin
America who shall henceforth live on in the hearts of Angolan
women.

127

Many of them have expressed their intention to support and take part in the forthcoming Conference of Solidarity with the Frontline States.

Many of them have reminded the Congress of the great threat to world peace represented by the armaments policy of imperialist circles who want to establish medium-range missiles in Europe, increasing the probability of a new world war, with disastrous consequences for humanity. This Congress, therefore, has also become a great forum of peace- and progress-loving forces.

To all those delegations we extend the thanks of the MPLA-Workers' Party, which will continue its unreserved support for the struggle of the fighting peoples of Namibia, South Africa, the Sahrawi Arab Democratic Republic, East Timor and El Salvador, all of them.

To all the friendly delegations we express our congratulations on International Women's Day, wishing them a good return home and full success in their work.

You have had occasion here to hear messages from OPA (Agostinho Neto Pioneers Organization), the Party Youth, UNTA and the defence and security forces. With the Party's support, may this serve as encouragement for the great programmes set by the Congress.

Most important among these programmes are those related to defence, cadre training, education, child care, and the production of goods for the whole population. The fulfilment of these tasks will be the surest contribution to achieving solid results in your struggle for emancipation and more just conditions for Angolan women and our pioneers.

To all of you and to all those, from Cabinda to the Cunene, who have helped to make the OMA Congress a success, we express our warmest and most fraternal congraulations.

We also congratulate the newly elected National Committee and Executive Secretariat, expressing sincere good wishes for success in your work and the effective strengthening of organization in every sphere. I should like here to congratulate Comrade Ruth Neto, re-elected as Secretary-General, and to wish her every success in her important post.

Long Live the OMA Congress!
For the Emancipation of Women
The Struggle Continues!
Victory is Certain!

128

PART THREE
Documents

7. Resolutions

Resolution on the Emancipation of Women

The First Congress of OMA made a detailed analysis of matters related to the Organization's internal life, particularly the functioning of its structures, and also studied the problem of the emancipation of women.

The First Congress concluded that for women to achieve equality and the full development of all their abilities, practical action must be taken to ensure their true and effective participation.

Profound changes in social, political and economic structures are the pre-condition for achieving equality in every sphere.

The fundamental changes required are the abolition of discrimination in legislation, the requisite legal guarantees for women freely to decide on their own future, enabling them to raise their educational level, choose the occupation they want, take part in political life, decide on marriage or divorce and control the number of their children.

The Congress recognizes that peasant women have through the ages been the most exploited and that they have least enjoyed social change. It therefore considers it indispensable that their consciousness be heightened with a view to their increased integration in co-operative work, so that they may benefit more from literacy campaigns, health education work and any technical changes likely to ease their hard work.

The First OMA Congress considers that to give meaning to the principle of equal opportunity to work, women must be able to exercise the right to general education, vocational training and technical advancement under the same conditions as men.

In view of the fact that education in the family and at school plays an important part in forming the personality of the young, enabling them to take decisions and solve their problems, the First OMA Congress urges all women in the countryside, towns, industry, agriculture, trade and administrative services to strive to increase their level of schooling, so that better work may lead to increased economic and social development.

The First OMA Congress urges women to practise sport, irrespective of their age, because women's involvement in sport has all kinds of beneficial effects, permitting not only better comradely relations but better psychological and physical equilibrium. Among its other tasks, therefore, OMA must mobilize mothers to encourage their children to practise sport at school.

The First OMA Congress considers it important to pay more attention to young working women, educating them politically and ideologically, so that they may in future be women dedicated to the cause of the revolution.

The Congress has noted that the struggle for the emancipation of women depends of necessity on their participation in the tasks of national reconstruction. On analysing the problems of housewives, it has been noted that the domestic economy is essential to the functioning of the economic system. This function of women is often underestimated, which is one of the factors leading to discrimination and the exclusion of women from active labour.

The First Congress considers that the problems of women not fully participating in every sphere of national reconstruction stem from a low schooling level and the lack of support for working women.

After examining in detail the problems of national defence, the Congress recognized the important role of the mothers of those of military age in encouraging them to join the army.

The First Congress regards it as extremely important, at this specific historical moment, that Angolan women, from Cabinda to the Cunene, should show their firm readiness to join the fighting forces, in order to face up to the war imposed on the People's Republic of Angola and to strengthen their internationalist stand in support of the just struggle of oppressed peoples throughout the world, especially in

Southern Africa.

Resolution on Working Women

1. Considering the important part women play in national
    reconstruction, the First Congress of OMA reaffirms
    the need to enforce the equality between men and
    women at work provided for in the laws of the Angolan
    State.

2. Considering that women should in practice enjoy the
    same opportunities as men, assume equal responsibilities
    and have the same rights, in accordance with their
    abilities, respecting and protecting their right to mother-
    hood and to support in vocational training, OMA
    should:

2.1 Co-operate closely with bodies in different sectors
    entrusted with the training of cadres, to ensure that a
    greater number of women have access to refresher
    courses, further training and education, also at their
    workplace.

2.2 Pay special attention to working women in rural areas
    and, whenever necessary, approach the local authorities
    with a view to guaranteeing and facilitating equal
    opportunities to study and to hold responsible and
    decision-making posts.

2.3 Urge employers to prevent pregnant women from
    carrying out activities which might harm the health of
    mother and child.

2.4 Participate in the training of cadres for mother-and-child
    care centres.

2.5 Consider with the appropriate authorities the opening
    hours of shops, so as to facilitate the purchase of goods,
    particularly foodstuffs, by working mothers, and call
    for the setting up of consumer co-operatives at work-
    places.

2.6 Contribute to an examination of the opening of auto-
    matic laundries, school and workplace canteens and

industrial kitchens, in order to increase social support for working mothers in urban areas and to minimize their domestic tasks.

2.7   Give fresh impetus to creating conditions to relieve peasant women, making use of some of the natural resources in their communities by such means as boring and protecting drinking water wells, promoting charcoal dealers' associations, building collective laundries, and encouraging the production of clay kitchen equipment and handicrafts.

2.8   Continue to recruit and organize traditional midwives.

2.9   Co-operate with the appropriate authorities in opening creches, nurseries and kindergartens at workplaces, in neighbourhoods and in agricultural co-operatives.

2.10 Take part in the implementation of the recommendations of the Workshop on Children regarding the problems of mother-and-child care, and mobilize the community for this work.

2.11 Participate with OPA and other appropriate bodies in occupying children's leisure time with sports and recreational and cultural activities in places that provide such facilities. Where no such structures exist, OMA and OPA shall consider practical means of solving the problem.

2.12 Give priority to functional literacy, particularly in rural areas, supporting the recruitment of people in their own areas to swell the ranks of literacy teachers, while providing them with incentives, because this is the only way to create conditions for involving women in work.

3.   In view of the fact that Article 158 of the General Labour Law provides for three months' pre- and post-natal leave for working mothers, and noting irregularities on the part of some women, OMA calls on women to show understanding and awareness and not to misuse this right to the detriment of the national reconstruction process.

4.   Considering that the inherent tasks of the home should

be shared by the couple, OMA recommends that Article
155 of the General Labour Law be revised, since it
conflicts with equal rights for men and women. It also
recommends that the list referred to in Article 154 be
drawn up and that OMA be included in the co-operation
referred to in paragraph 2 of that article.

5.   Mobilize women to be exemplary in their work sectors
in fulfilling the tasks and targets set by the Emergency
Programmes and General Emergency Plan.

Resolution on Women and the Family

Considering that the State and society have a fundamental
responsibility with regard to the development of the family,
especially for educating children in a new morality;

The First Congress of the Organization of Angolan Women
(OMA), meeting from 2 to 8 March 1983, adopts the following resolution:

1.   It is necessary to speed up the drafting of new legislation
on the family which ensures equality between men and
women, defends the interests of children and contributes
to the establishment of a new family morality.

2.   New information and guidance services must be created
to help women defend their rights.

3.   All the country's leading bodies must be made responsible for publicizing and implementing new guidelines
on the family, especially as regards non-discrimination
and equal rights and duties.

4.   State bodies should create conditions to ensure greater
protection and equality for children, whether born in
wedlock or not, so that within the family and society
they may attain full physical and psychological development, and that their schooling efforts may strengthen
the bonds between the family and society.

5.   In the case of children born out of wedlock, special
      attention should be paid to the establishment and
      payment of allowances for the children and, if need be,
      for the women, directly deducting the allowance from
      the father's pay.

6.   The running of juvenile courts needs to be improved,
      and specialized courts should be set up in every province
      to deal with matters related to the family and minors.

7.   A careful study should be made of the effects of the
      legal presumption of paternity of the mother's husband,
      if they are separated but not divorced, and new legisla-
      tion should be drawn up on this question.

8.   The appropriate bodies, particularly the Ministry of
      Justice, should take the necessary measures to ensure
      that the marriage ceremony is performed with the
      solemnity inherent in the act, with regard to the registry
      office, the training of its officials and the marriage
      formalities.

9.   Legal and social measures should be taken to protect
      unmarried mothers, and the family allowance for a
      woman or man who has to bring up a child alone should
      be reviewed.

10.   Steps should be taken to protect the rights of a woman
      whose relationship with a man is the result not of
      marriage but of a *de facto* union.

11.   Conditions should be created for young women to study
      in order to acquire vocational training and to ensure
      that they have the necessary economic independence.
      It is important to organize meetings of young people,
      under the guidance of the Party, OMA and the JMPLA-
      Party Youth, to discuss matters related to courtship,
      marriage and sex.

12.   Conditions should be created at all levels to ensure the
      right of women to freely consented motherhood. The
      fulfilment of that right calls for the creation of facilities

for sex education, particularly in schools, using the mass media to provide information on family planning and the use of contraceptive methods.

13. Efforts should be made to educate parents and relatives with a view to ensuring that young girls who become pregnant are not forced to marry against their will or against the will of the boy.

14. Traditionalist ideas on the fertility of women need to be combated, and the commission already set up to implement a family planning programme should start work immediately, as one of the ways of reducing infant mortality.

15. As a last resort, in an unwanted pregnancy which could harm the physical, mental or social welfare of a woman or girl, abortion should be authorized, bearing in mind the recommendations of the World Health Organization.

16. There should be frank discussions on the problems of prostitution, making an in-depth study of its causes, so as to make society aware of the need to eradicate this cancer. Schools should be called upon to take part in such discussions, in order to be able to provide better guidance in educating students for life.

17. Meetings, talks, symposia and so forth should be held with a view to the continuous education of adults on the new relationships in the family and society.

18. All discriminatory measures and attitudes towards women should cease in State services, especially that of requesting a husband's permission for a woman to travel, and it should be compulsory to obtain the mother's permission for children to go abroad.

Resolution on OMA Statutes

In view of the fact that the founding of OMA was a result of the need for women to participate in an organized way in the Angolan people's independence struggle led by the MPLA, and of the need for their complete emancipation, by engaging in the tasks of the revolution and the building of socialism;

Considering that the draft statutes have been amply studied by militants in local branches of OMA who have put forward suggestions to improve their content;

The First Congress of the Organization of Angolan Women adopts the following resolution:

1. It calls upon all members to study the Statutes and scrupulously abide by the principles of democratic centralism and unity within OMA.

2. It entrusts the National Committee of OMA, on the basis of the Statutes, to draw up all the regulations required for their practical implementation at every level of the Organization and in all its activities.

    Unity, Organization, Development
    For the Emancipation of Women
    The Struggle Continues!
    Victory is Certain!

Luanda, 7 March 1983
Year of Strengthened Organization

8. Statutes of the Organization of Angolan Women

CHAPTER I
Definition and purposes

Article 1
The Organization of Angolan Women, OMA, shall be an organization for all Angolan women, irrespective of their political or religious beliefs, who are fighting for complete emancipation and for involvement in the tasks of the revolution and building socialism.

Article 2
OMA shall carry out its activities with a view to women's full participation in the country's political, economic and social life, constantly striving to raise their educational and cultural level.

Article 3
OMA, within the framework of the principles of the MPLA-Workers' Party, shall educate women in the spirit of love for their country, scientific socialism and proletarian internationalism.

Article 4
OMA shall aim to develop a new mentality among Angolan women, combating all reactionary attitudes, particularly regionalism, tribalism, racism, obscurantism and all vices inherited from capitalist colonial society.

CHAPTER II
Membership, duties, rights and sanctions

Article 5
Membership of OMA shall be open to all Angolan women
over 16 who accept its Statutes and who fight consistently
for the attainment of its objectives.

Article 6
Membership of OMA shall be voluntary and individual. In
order to join, a candidate shall make an oral application to
the appropriate OMA branch, and admission shall be approved
by the secretariat of the branch and later ratified by an
assembly of branch members.

Article 7
1. The duties of an OMA member shall be as follows:
(a) To know and abide by the Organization's Statutes and
strive to ensure that they are implemented.
(b) To set an example at work and strive constantly to raise
her political, educational and vocational level.
(c) To take an active part in all meetings of OMA bodies,
respecting established working methods and fulfilling all the
tasks entrusted to her.
(d) To take an active part in the country's political, economic
and social life, helping to strengthen the national economy,
defence and security, and to raise the people's educational
and cultural level.
(e) To be honest and true to the people and the revolution,
and to place the interests of the masses of the people before
all personal interests.
(f) Regularly to pay the dues set by the Organization.

2. Members holding leading posts shall set an example of
modesty and loyalty, constantly concerning themselves with
the problems faced by grassroots branches of the Organization
and always bearing in mind that such posts do not imply
privilege but greater sacrifice and responsibility.

Article 8
An OMA member shall enjoy the following rights:
(a) To elect or be elected to leading bodies, or to be a delegate

to any meeting or congress.
(b) To take part in meetings of the Organization, freely
expressing her views on any matter and contributing to the
decisions taken.
(c) To examine within the body to which she belongs the work
of the Organization, and if need be to criticize the work of
higher bodies and the activity of the Organization or of any
member.
(d) To submit to higher OMA bodies, through the body to
which she belongs, any matters regarded as being of interest
to the Organization.
(e) Not to be punished without a hearing.
(f) To take part in seminars, refresher courses and the various
activities organized by OMA.

Article 9
It shall be the duty and right of OMA members to use criticism
and self-criticism as a means of combating errors and
improving working methods. Criticism, which should always
be made within the Organization's structures and in a fraternal
way, shall always be aimed at re-educating the member at
fault. Self-criticism shall not be formal but conscious, and it
should be followed in practice by the correction of errors
made.

Article 10
A member of the Organization who violates the Statutes,
decisions, resolutions or norms, or whose unworthy behaviour
is prejudicial to OMA's name and prestige, shall be subject to
the disciplinary sanctions provided for in the present Statutes.

Article 11
The disciplinary sanctions shall be as follows:
(a) Personal censure.
(b) Public censure
(c) Suspension of membership for a maximum period of one
year.
(d) Expulsion.

Article 12
1. Personal censure shall be made by the branch secretariat
and shall not be recorded in the member's curriculum vitae.

2. Public censure shall take place at a meeting of branch members.

3. The sanctions referred to in paragraphs (c) and (d) of the foregoing article shall be the responsibility of the body superior to that to which the defaulting member belongs, and expulsion shall be ratified by the OMA National Committee.

Article 13

1. The application of sanctions, except in cases of personal censure, shall be preceded by an enquiry to establish the facts, at which the defaulting member shall have a hearing. Sanctions shall be imposed after a detailed examination of the accusations made and of the defence presented, bearing in mind the seriousness of the fault and the responsibility of the member who committed it.

2. Disciplinary sanctions should not be seen merely as punishment, but as a way to re-educate the defaulting member, bearing in mind the strengthened unity and cohesion of the Organization.

3. Any decision to impose sanctions, apart from personal censure, shall allow of appeal to a higher body.

CHAPTER III
Structure and working methods

Article 14
OMA shall be structured with the following echelons:
— National.
— Provincial.
— Municipal.
— Communal.
— Neighbourhood or village.

Article 15
The base OMA organization, in urban neighbourhoods and rural villages, shall be the branch, run by a secretariat.

Article 16
The fundamental working method within the Organization shall be democratic centralism. In accordance with this principle, OMA's work shall be based on the following:

(a) The election of all leading bodies from top to base.
(b) The subordination of lower bodies to higher bodies.
(c) The obligation of lower bodies regularly to inform and report on their activities to higher bodies, whose decisions shall be mandatory.
(d) The obligation of higher bodies to report to those who elected them.
(e) The free discussion of OMA problems within each body. After decisions have been taken, they shall be mandatory for all members of the body, and the minority shall have to abide by the decision of the majority.
(f) The practice of the principle of collective leadership, which shall not rule out individual responsibility for carrying out tasks decided upon.
(g) The practice of criticism and self-criticism and frank discussion, with a view to correcting errors and strengthening the Organization.

CHAPTER IV
OMA's Higher and Leading Bodies

Article 17
OMA's organs at national level shall be:
(a) Congress.
(b) National Committee.
(c) National Executive Secretariat.

Article 18
Leading organs at provincial, municipal and communal level shall be:
(a) Assembly of members.
(b) Committee.
(c) Executive Secretariat.

Article 19
The leading organs at all levels shall be democratically elected by the Congress and assemblies.

Article 20
Procedures for the election of delegates to the Congress and assemblies shall be laid down in regulations to be drawn up

by the OMA National Committee.

CHAPTER V
Leading organs of OMA at National Level

The Congress

Article 21
The Congress shall be the highest leading organ of OMA and shall meet in ordinary session every five years.

Article 22
The Congress shall be convened by the National Committee of OMA at least six months in advance. If need be, the National Committee may convene special congresses with at least two months' notice.

Article 23
The Congress shall consider that its meetings are valid when, through the delegates, at least two-thirds of the members of OMA are represented.

Article 24
The Congress shall:
(a) Assess, discuss and approve the report on the Organization's activities presented by the National Committee.
(b) Discuss and draw up in broad outline the activities to be carried out by the Organization until the following Congress.
(c) Discuss, amend and adopt the OMA Statutes.
(d) Elect members of the National Committee.

The National Committee

Article 25
The National Committee shall be the highest leading organ of OMA which shall guide all the Organization's activities between congresses.

Article 26
The National Committee shall be elected by the Congress from among members proposed by the Organization's provincial assemblies.

Article 27
The National Committee shall meet in ordinary session twice
yearly, and in special session when convened by the National
Secretariat or by two-thirds of the members of the National
Committee.

Article 28
The National Committee shall:
(a) See to the fulfilment of the guidelines laid down by the
Congress, taking whatever measures are required to ensure
that they are fulfilled.
(b) Direct and supervise all OMA's activities, helping the
various bodies to perform their tasks.
(c) Discuss and approve all documents and proposals presented
to the Congress, and undertake such studies on matters
related to women as are necessary for the fulfilment of OMA's
objectives.
(d) Support the structure of OMA bodies at all levels and
draw up the regulations required for their activity.
(e) Regularly inform the various echelons of the Organization
of the work being done.
(f) Elect from among its members the Secretary-General and
members of the National Executive Secretariat.
(g) Propose new members of the National Committee.
(h) Establish procedures of representation and the election of
delegates to the Congress and provincial, municipal and
communal assemblies.
(i) Define OMA's position on national and international events.
(j) Establish the guidelines for OMA's international work.
(k) Approve OMA's budget and the allocation of funds.

The National Executive Secretariat

Article 29
The National Executive Secretariat shall be the organ that
directs OMA's activities between meetings of the National
Committee.

Article 30
The National Executive Secretariat shall comprise the
Secretary-General and the secretaries selected by OMA's
National Committee.

Article 31
The National Executive Secretariat shall:
(a) Direct, organize and supervise the fulfilment of the guidelines laid down by the Congress and the National Committee.
(b) Give impetus to OMA's work in order to mobilize Angolan women to take part in all tasks that further their true emancipation.
(c) Inform the National Committee of the progress made in the Organization's work.
(d) Make proposals to the National Committee on ways of constantly improving the Organization's activity.
(e) Meet periodically, in accordance with the regulations.

The Secretary-General

Article 32
1. The Secretary-General shall:
(a) Direct, guide and supervise the activities of OMA's various bodies and give impetus to their work.
(b) Guide and co-ordinate the work of the Secretariats.
(c) Preside over meetings of the National Committee and the National Executive Secretariat.
(d) Represent and speak in the name of OMA nationally and internationally.
(e) Delegate her functions, whenever necessary, to another member of the National Executive Secretariat.

2. When voting takes place, the Secretary-General shall be entitled to have a casting vote.

Secretariats

Article 33
The Secretariats shall co-ordinate the respective departments of the National Executive Secretariat.

CHAPTER VI
Leading organs at provincial, municipal and communal level

Article 34
Assemblies of members at provincial, municipal and communal

level shall be the highest OMA organs at those echelons.

Article 35
1. The assemblies shall be composed of members of the committee at that level and delegates elected by assemblies at the immediately lower level.

2. Communal assemblies shall include, in addition to members of the communal committee, delegates elected by the branches.

Article 36
Provincial, municipal and communal assemblies shall:
(a) Examine and discuss reports presented by the committee at the respective echelon.
(b) Lay down guidelines for the implementation, within the prescribed time, of decisions and work programmes adopted by higher bodies of OMA.
(c) Elect the members of the committee at that echelon.
(d) Propose candidates to the committee at the immediately higher echelon.

Article 37
Provincial, municipal and communal assemblies shall meet in ordinary session once yearly, and in special session when convened by the respective committee at least one month in advance.

Provincial, municipal and communal committees

Article 38
1. Provincial, municipal and communal committees shall be elected by assemblies at the relevant level from among members proposed by the assemblies of immediately lower echelons.

2. The number of members of committees at different echelons shall be determined in special regulations of the National Committee.

Article 39
Provincial, municipal and communal committees shall:

(a) Direct the Organization's activity between assemblies.
(b) Take the decisions required for the proper running of the various bodies.
(c) Elect from among their members the members of the Executive Secretariats.
(d) Regularly inform the different echelons of the work being done.
(e) Prepare studies and proposals to be presented to higher bodies, with a view to strengthening the Organization's activity.

Provincial, municipal and communal secretariats

Article 40
The Executive Secretariats shall be permanent organs that direct the Organization's activity at the respective echelons between meetings of the committee.

Article 41
Provincial, municipal and communal secretariats shall include the provincial, municipal or communal secretary and the number of secretaries to be established by the National Committee.

Article 42
The provincial, municipal and communal secretariats shall, at their respective echelon:
(a) Give impetus to the Organization's activity.
(b) Direct, guide and supervise the fulfilment of guidelines drawn up by the assemblies and committees.
(c) Co-ordinate and guide the activity of the Organization between meetings of the respective committees.
(d) Make proposals to the committees on measures to be taken to improve the Organization's work

Provincial, municipal and communal secretaries

Article 43
Provincial, municipal and communal secretaries shall, at their respective echelon:
(a) Guide and supervise the activities of their respective body.
(b) Co-ordinate and supervise the work of the secretariats.
(c) Preside over meetings of the committees and Executive

Secretariats.
(d) Delegate their functions, whenever necessary, to another member of the Executive Secretariat.

CHAPTER VII
Branches

Article 44
Branches shall be the OMA base organizations, functioning at neighbourhood or village level.

Article 45
The branch shall be composed of all the OMA members at that level and shall meet once a month.

Article 46
Branches shall:
(a) Discuss the branch work programme and take measures to ensure that it is efficiently implemented.
(b) Publicize the aims and decisions of OMA among women in their area.
(c) Co-operate with the Party, the State and other mass and social organizations to mobilize women to fulfil necessary tasks.
(d) Organize women in their area to fulfil programmed tasks, especially those related to literacy teaching, and helping with vaccination campaigns, health education, children's homes, creches and schools.
(e) Contribute to the Organization's constant growth, mobilizing particularly housewives in their area and women whose work has been most outstanding.
(f) Contribute to the development of the attitude towards women's production in urban areas, combating absenteeism, unpunctuality, indiscipline and a lack of interest in work.
(g) See to the civic, cultural and ideological education of their members, striving progressively to involve women in all sectors of national life.
(h) Constantly to sound the feelings of the masses of the people and inform higher bodies of the situation in their area.
(i) Make proposals to higher bodies with a view to constantly improving the Organization's work.

(j) Elect from among their members the branch Secretary and Secretariat.

(k) Regularly collect members' dues.

Branch Secretariats

Article 47
The leading organ of OMA at branch level shall be the Secretariat, elected by an assembly of members.

Article 48
1. The Secretariat shall be the permanent body of the branch and shall be structured in accordance with the present Statutes and the guidelines of the National Committee, bearing in mind the specific situation in each neighbourhood or village.

2. The Secretariat, under the leadership of the Secretary, shall supervise the fulfilment of all guidelines and work programmes adopted by the Organization.

CHAPTER VIII
Membership of international organizations

Article 49
Whenever it deems it appropriate to do so, OMA may join international organizations whose principles accord with those of OMA.

CHAPTER IX

Article 50
OMA's funds shall accrue essentially from members' dues and various contributions, subsidies and earnings.

CHAPTER X

Article 51
The symbols of OMA shall be its Flag, Emblem and Anthem.

(a) The OMA Flag shall be a red rectangle, with the Organization's Emblem in the centre, having the following dimensions:

Length ....120 cm
Width ....80 cm
Emblem radius ....20 cm

(b) The OMA Emblem shall be a circle on a red background inside which there shall be a black silhouette of a woman with a rifle on her shoulder, and the inscription in yellow — ORGANIZAÇÃO DA MULHER ANGOLANA — OMA.

CHAPTER XI
Amendments to the Statutes and dissolution of OMA

Article 52
Only the OMA Congress shall have the authority to replace, revise or amend the Statutes.

Article 53
OMA may be dissolved only be a decision of the Congress. In that event all its assets shall revert to the State.

CHAPTER XII
Omissions

Article 54
Any omission from the present Statutes shall be made good by decision of OMA's National Committee.